Gender and Mathematics

An International Perspective

Edited by
Leone Burton

CASSELL

Cassell Educational Limited
Villiers House
41/47 Strand
WC2N 5JE

First published 1990
Reprinted 1992

British Library Cataloguing in Publication Data
Gender and mathematics.
   1. Mathematics
   1. Burton, Leone
   510

   ISBN 0-304-32279-2

Typeset by Colset Private Limited, Singapore
Printed and bound by Short Run Press Ltd., Exeter

Contents

Acknowledgements

This book is the outcome of the Women and Mathematics Topic Area at the Sixth International Congress on Mathematics Education held in Budapest, Hungary, in 1988. The preparation of those sessions and, more generally, the work of the International Organization of Women and Mathematics Education (IOWME) was aided by a generous grant from Unesco and the Editor of this volume would like to express her gratitude, in particular, to Ed Jacobsen for his support.

The book is dedicated to future generations of women in all parts of the world in the hope that they will be able to benefit from conditions of equality of opportunity that will render redundant further considerations of gender bias.

Notes on the Contributors

Mary Barnes is Director of the Mathematics Learning Centre at the University of Sydney, New South Wales, Australia. This Centre aims to increase access to mathematics-based courses by providing a variety of forms of assistance and support to disadvantaged students. Mary's main areas of interest are the teaching and learning of calculus and the role of gender in mathematics education. She is currently working on a project to develop gender-inclusive curriculum materials for the teaching of calculus.

Joanne Rossi Becker is a full professor in the Department of Mathematics and Computer Science at San Jose State University, California, USA where she teaches pre-service and in-service courses in mathematics and mathematics education for teachers. Her areas of research interest include gender and mathematics and teacher education in mathematics.

Leone Burton edited *Girls into Maths Can Go*, the first book to be published in the UK specifically addressing issues of gender and mathematics learning. Concerned about social images of mathematics and the resultant quality of mathematics learning, she has researched aspects of enquiry-based learning in the primary, secondary and tertiary sectors always, her son maintains, just that bit too late to help him! She is the author of *Thinking Things Through* and co-authored *Thinking Mathematically*. She is a member of a team which has produced the first thematically based mathematics scheme for primary schools, published by Harcourt, Brace, Jovanovich. Professionally involved with the pre-service and in-service education of teachers, she is Professor of Education (Mathematics and Science) at the University of Birmingham, UK. She was Convenor of the International Organization of Women and Mathematics Education from 1984 to 1988.

Mary Coupland is a mathematics teacher who has worked with school students, trainee teachers, adult learners and undergraduates. She is active in the Mathematical Association of New South Wales, including their Special Interest Group for Girls and Mathematics. She is currently lecturing in the School of Mathematical Sciences at the University of Technology, Sydney, New South Wales, Australia.

Giuseppina Fenaroli is a graduate in mathematics and works in the Department of Mathematics at the University of Genoa in Italy. She researches in the history and foundations of probability and statistics.

Fulvia Furinghetti is associate professor of mathematics at the University of Genoa in Italy. She is responsible for the Research Group in Mathematics Education at Genoa University which is supported by a grant from the Italian National Research Council. She has organized courses for the training of mathematics teachers, authored papers in mathematics education, history of mathematics, and algebraic geometry and edited books in mathematics education and in the history of mathematics.

Antonio Garibaldi is a former Professor of Mathematical Physics and is currently Professor of the History of Mathematics. His fields of interest include the history of algebra, probability and applied mathematics in the sixteenth to the nineteenth centuries.

Gila Hanna is an associate professor in the Department of Measurement, Evaluation and Computer Applications at the Ontario Institute for Studies in Education, Toronto, Canada. Her research and teaching interests are data analysis and statistics and mathematics education. She is Convenor of the International Organization of Women and Mathematics Education for the years 1988–1992.

Sue Helme has been involved in adult education since 1981, with a commitment to building women's confidence in their ability to learn mathematics. She established a return to study programme for women at Broadmeadows College of Technical and Further Education in Melbourne, Australia, which is designed to encourage women to proceed with studies in mathematics and science. She co-authored *Mathematics: a New Beginning* and is involved in staff development programmes for adult basic education teachers.

Zelda Isaacson is a freelance educational consultant, writer and lecturer, having formerly been Senior Lecturer in Mathematics Education at the Polytechnic of North London, in the UK. She founded GAMMA (the Gender and Mathematics Association of the UK) in 1981 and has written extensively on the subject of gender and mathematics. She is author of the book *Teaching GSCE Mathematics*.

Berinderjeet Kaur is currently a lecturer in the Mathematics Education Department of the Institute of Education in Singapore. She is also the national representative for Singapore of the International Organization for Women and Mathematics Education for the years 1988–1992.

Erika Kündiger is an associate professor at the University of Windsor, Canada. She is the editor of the book *An International Review on Gender and Mathematics*, ERIC, 1982 and has published numerous articles on women and mathematics and motivational aspects of teaching and learning mathematics.

Christine Larouche was formerly a graduate student in the Department of Measurement, Evaluation and Computer Applications at the Ontario Institute for Studies in Education, Toronto, Canada. She has recently interrupted her programme to pursue independent studies with a view towards gaining a broad picture of the direction of science in the future. For this purpose, she is presently delving into a number of different disciplines, ranging from astrophysics to philosophy.

Gilah Leder is an Associate Professor in the Faculty of Education at Monash University, Melbourne, Australia. She is interested in all aspects of mathematics education, particularly gender differences, the impact of affective components on mathematics learning, and exceptionality. She has published widely in each of these areas. She recently completed two books: *Mathematics and Gender*, with Elizabeth Fennema, and *Educating Girls: Practice and Research*, with Shirley Sampson.

Beth Marr has been active in the feminist women's movement in Melbourne, Victoria, Australia for many years. She was involved in the establishment of a women's refuge and a co-operative women's press. She has taught in adult education for ten years where she has concentrated on the mathematics education of adult women returning to study. This has involved development of curricula, teaching and in-servicing other teachers, as well as the co-ordination of a team of 15 women teachers in the Teaching Maths to Women Project. She co-authored *Mathematics: A New Beginning*. Beth is currently working at Northern Metropolitan College of TAFE, Preston, Victoria 3072, Australia.

Prudence Purser is currently Senior Dean at Burnside High School, New Zealand's largest secondary school. As well as teaching mathematics, she is also an author of several mathematics textbooks for secondary school students which are widely used throughout the country. This contact with secondary school students has produced a desire to see girls achieve their full potential in mathematics. She is currently National Co-ordinator of the New Zealand branch of IOWME.

Máire Rodgers is a lecturer in Mathematics Education at the University of Ulster at Coleraine, Northern Ireland. She works with both pre-service and in-service teachers and has previously taught in second-level schools in Northern Ireland and the Republic of Ireland. Her interests include issues of equity in the classroom and the development of co-operative modes of learning.

Pat Rogers lives in Toronto, Canada, with her daughter, Kate. She has a PhD in Mathematics from the University of London and presently teaches Mathematics at York University, Ontario, where she is also the Director of the Centre for the Support of Teaching. Pat is currently involved in classroom research in feminist pedagogy and mathematics.

Anna Somaglia is a teacher of mathematics and physics in an Italian senior secondary school (state scientific lyceum). She does research in the history of mathematics.

Lyn Taylor is an Assistant Professor of Mathematics Education at the University of Colorado-Denver, USA. In 1989–1991 she is serving as President of Women and

Mathematics Education (USA). The focus of her scholarship is mathematical attitudes, particularly from a Vygotskian perspective. Presently she is involved in projects examining the mathematical attitudes of elementary teachers and middle school American Indian students.

Evangelie Tressou-Milonas completed her pre-graduate education in Greece and her professional training and doctorate at Leicester University in the UK. She now works in the Department of Primary Education of the Aristotle University of Thessaloniki in Greece.

Heleen Verhage works at the OW & OC research group on mathematics education at the State University of Utrecht, The Netherlands. She is involved with curriculum development for upper and lower secondary level. Until the next ICME in 1992, she is the Editor of the IOWME Newsletter.

Helen Wily, now retired, has been Head of Mathematics at a secondary school, author of several mathematics resource books and, latterly, Senior Lecturer in Mathematics Education at the Christchurch College of Education. In 1985, she founded the New Zealand branch of IOWME. One of the early New Zealand investigators into gender differences in mathematics, she has published several research papers and recently a bibliography of New Zealand work relevant to gender and mathematics.

NB. Any author whose address is not specified can be contacted through the Editor.

International Organisation of Women and Mathematics Education
The International Organisation of Women and Mathematics Education came into being at ICME 4, 1980, Berkeley, USA, as a result of a preliminary meeting at ICME 3, 1976 which discussed 'Women and Mathematics'. Since 1987, IOWME has been an affiliated study group of the International Commission on Mathematical Instruction (ICMI).

IOWME is an international network of individuals and groups who share a commitment to equity in education and are interested in the links between gender and the learning and teaching of mathematics. It is organized through a structure consisting of a Convenor and Newsletter Editor, elected at a business meeting held during ICME Congresses. In addition, there are National Co-ordinators, elected or appointed, who organize local IOWME activities and distribute the *IOWME Newsletter*.

The aims of IOWME are:

1. to provide a forum for those interested in the relationship between gender and mathematics;
2. to provide current information on research and curriculum development concerning gender and mathematics;
3. to encourage and disseminate research related to:
   (a) women's participation in mathematics, science and technology;
   (b) factors influencing participation rates and the quality of teaching mathematics, science and technology;
   (c) strategies and programmes designed to increase the participation of women in the mathematical sciences.

Introduction

Leone Burton

The performance of Oxbridge women in university examinations has declined since the advent of mixed colleges. Despite a considerable increase in the number of women under-graduates at Oxford from 16% in the mid-1960s to the current 40%, the gap between the proportion of women and men getting firsts has widened. According to the *Oxford Review of Education*: 'While the number of women studying in each university has risen nearly to parity with men, and while all colleges but a few traditionally reserved for women admit both men and women, who are taught (presumably) in the same circumstances, proportionally fewer women have achieved first class honours and few have found themselves in the third class.'
(Report in *The Times Higher Education Supplement*, 16 February 1990, p. 1.)

The above report serves to draw attention, yet again, to five aspects of the gender and education debate that have been addressed in the research literature. The first three relate to counting heads: first, the numerical presence of females and males; second, the subject distribution of the females and males, implicitly above but dealt with more explicitly in the mathematics education literature; and, third, the success rate of women in comparison with men. The fourth aspect concerns the climate within which learning takes place; in particular, the impact of single-sex or mixed-sex classes. Finally, the report makes the assumption so often encountered that students *can* be offered the 'same' experience, despite a growing literature which challenges this.

The proportion of women gaining qualifications within the education systems of many countries has indeed been rising but the subject distribution of these qualifi-cations, and ultimately of the career pathways that they open, continues to be biased. There is need for a cross-cultural database, which would demonstrate how these numbers are changing not only in global terms but also in terms of subject distribution. If one society demonstrates different experiences from another, lessons need to be generalized. Unfortunately, at present, these data are not available. However, we do have the data from the Second International Mathematics Study and, in this volume, Gila Hanna and her colleagues present the results of their analysis of sex differences at the end of secondary school in the 15 participating countries.

Success curves in different subject areas do not match for gender, nor over time. In the UK in mathematics, for example, males are overrepresented at both ends of the gradings obtained at the end of compulsory schooling and this appears to be the case reported above more generally for university students at Oxbridge. However, in language and literature study, the gender distribution looks very different. And the advent of new subject disciplines, such as computer science in the UK, appeared to offer opportunities to women students that were rejected once the discipline became established within the power complex of mathematics/science/technology. Courses that attracted healthy percentages of women up to five years ago now have all-male intakes. To what degree will this experience be replicated in those societies only now beginning to introduce computer science as a discrete discipline area? Can they make use of the longer-term experiences of others?

Where education systems offer the choice of either single-sex or mixed-sex organization, research has indicated that the former appears to favour females, the latter not to prejudice males. The point is made in the above report: as numbers have increased and colleges have moved to mixed-sex intakes, women's degree results have tended to the middle. The observation begs many questions. Surely a change in social groupings does not affect women's abilities although there is ample evidence that it does affect their achievement. Both the observation and the causes for it demand investigation world-wide, particularly as the movement towards mixed-sex schooling is perceived in many societies as more *socially* appropriate and more *educationally* liberating.

The author of the *Oxford Review* article makes a presumption that would be disputed by the results of many studies undertaken during the past ten years. This is that the teaching offered to men and women is experienced 'in the same circumstances'. Indeed, those espousing a constructivist position in education would claim that it is impossible for any two learners to construe the 'same' learning experience in the same way. Add to this the differential messages carried for females and males by the social, political and personal contexts that are part of the circumstances within which learning is set and the absurdity of that 'presumably' is underlined. Nonetheless, many educators continue to operate under the mistaken assumption that equivalence of outcomes is assured by ignoring differences ('I concentrate on the student and do not notice their sex, race, etc.'), by offering the same 'treatment' to all ('They all use the same textbook so they have equal chances to succeed') or by declaring an equal opportunities intent without investigating and exposing the implications of this for institutional roles and for teacher, student and parental behaviour ('We are an equal opportunities institution').

Research increasingly underlines for us how misguided these positions are. Many investigators have examined the classroom as a sociopolitical setting within which differential messages are given and received by different groups of students. Research in some cultures has established that even teachers who are determined to treat students equally find that the males can manipulate them into a greater number of contacts. Equally, other studies have established that the quality of interactions between teacher and male students is different from that with female students. In many classrooms, there is a failure to recognize that scarce resources become the focus of a perceived power battle within which possession of the scarce resource can connote a victory. In this respect, the teacher is a scarce resource. Equally, the same phenomenon can be seen at work with the computer—another scarce resource. Avoiding the conditions under which this happens requires considerable thought and the deliberate application of chosen strategies. The literature is not overwhelmed with comparative studies which investigate differences in gender responses under differently chosen conditions of learning where this issue of power is, or is not, challenged.

Although the links between gender and the learning and teaching of mathematics have, recently, been an important focus of attention in the USA and, to a lesser extent, in Australia, Canada and the UK, those concerned about this relationship in other societies have been more marginalized and without easy access to publication. Their work has fallen into two distinct categories: causal relationships established in, say, the USA, have been investigated to see if they are observable under different cultural conditions; new and different perspectives have been adopted to inform the national and the international debate. Both strands are present in this volume which also spans the different phases of education from primary schooling right through to university. The 'big four', Australia, Canada, the UK and the USA still dominate but the presence of contributions from Greece, Italy, The Netherlands, New Zealand, and Singapore demonstrates not only that the issue is one that is of concern outside the English-speaking developed world, and not only in countries with large and complex educational systems, but wherever women and men are educated within formal systems that control access to resources and success in society.

One example of a trend within which is embedded apparent contradiction can be found in a comparison of the Singapore with the New Zealand contributions. Berinderjeet Kaur draws attention to her significant finding confirming the American result that males outperformed females in statistics. On the other hand, Prue Purser and Helen Wily comment, from their data, that 'the high proportion of women engaged in statistical work is of interest'. In compiling a Directory of Women engaged in Mathematics, Statistics and Computer Science in the Universities and Polytechnics of the UK, I too found that women were more frequently engaged in teaching or researching in statistics than in other areas of mathematics. Of course, the comparison here is not unproblematic as women who complete higher education in mathematics and then choose to enter a statistical field present a different sample from school students completing their compulsory mathematical education. However, Berinderjeet Kaur draws attention to the sociopolitical context within which mathematics is taught and learned as a starting point for the analysis of this apparent contradiction.

This book is divided into four sections, Gender and Classroom Practice, Gender and the Curriculum, Gender and Achievement, and Women's Presence. These four sections represent the current state of the international debate in mathematics education. The first section, Gender and Classroom Practice reflects the considerable amount of work that has been done or is currently in progress on the climate within which mathematics education is encountered and its effects on those who are attempting to learn the discipline. Gilah Leder is one of the foremost researchers in this area and her chapter draws attention to the range of existing work, internationally, methodologically and in terms of research foci. Her conclusions leave no room for complacency: even in societies that have taken gender effects seriously, substantial shifts in teacher behaviour have not occurred. In referring to teachers' behaviours she says:

> It is certainly likely that they will contribute to and reinforce differences in girls' and boys' perceptions of themselves as learners of mathematics, perceptions which may ultimately be translated into differences in achievement and participation in mathematics.

Zelda Isaacson uses the declared experiences of mature women, who have come to a study of mathematics later and despite negative feelings about the discipline, to draw out implications for classroom practice. She records particular changes in attitudes in these women which, however, would not have been possible were it not for deliberate re-negotiation of the role of the teacher, the nature of mathematical activity and an emphasis on discussion within the context of collaborative groups.

The two chapters by Maire Rodgers and by Pat Rogers, look in closer detail at the effects on mathematics learning in attitudes towards learning of both negative and positive classroom experiences. Maire, in contrast to Zelda, talked with school students who had the option to choose further study in mathematics, and with their teachers. She collected their reasons for deciding whether or not to continue with the subject and, for those who did, how they felt about different parts of their course. In analys-ing the reasons which might explain the feelings that were expressed, she compares the students' experiences with those of parents and children choosing to attend out-of-school leisure mathematics classes. She makes the important point that, as learners, we are more likely to obtain satisfaction and pleasure from grappling successfully with something challenging than from being sucked through an educative process that removes anomalies, inconsistencies and 'difficulties' thereby sanitizing the content. She says:

> The learning situation must contain a fine balance of *sufficient* challenge and *sufficient* experience of success. Too much or too little of either can produce anxiety and mental paralysis or boredom and apathy.

Pat looked in detail at the classroom behaviour of one particular male teacher in a mathematics department whose female university students are highly successful. She points out that he has not chosen a role or styles of teaching which might particularly appeal to women students but deliberately invokes enquiry, discussion, collaborative work within a philosophy of mathematics education that relates to the negotiation of mathematical meaning and student empowerment, rather than the transmission of knowledge and skills. In describing this methodology, she says:

> The caring teacher trusts the student to grow in her own time and in her own way, and he is patient because he believes in and trusts in the student's ability to grow, to make mistakes and to learn from them. He will actively promote and safeguard conditions that are favour-able to his students' growth.

Lyn Taylor's chapter considers what personal and intellectual differences distinguish those who are successfully pursuing a university career, eight as professors of mathe-matics and four of social science. These are the women and men who have achieved mathematically and Lyn found that the female mathematicians are 'as confident mathematically and equally comfortable in social situations as the men', which she attributes to a changing social climate creating more opportunities. It would perhaps be possible to argue that the women who succeed in mathematics are more like the men who succeed than they are like other women! That is, that we are looking at a process of acculturization which remains unchallenged in the majority of classrooms and curricula offered to learners of mathematics.

The second section of the book, Gender and the Curriculum, confronts this issue of the nature of the curriculum. For too long mathematicians, female and male, have left unchallenged the assertion that mathematics is an international language which, by its abstract nature, cannot favour one group rather than another. Like most complex statements, there is both truth and falsehood in this. Certainly it is obvious that the language and culture of origin of a piece of presented mathematics are less likely to influence its comprehension by those who work in different languages or cultures than the clarity of argument through which its case is made. However, depersonalized and dehumanized mathematical argument is a stylized and conventionalized communicative device reified particularly in more recent centuries. Mathematics has not always been presented in this way but, more importantly, it is not devised in this way. Many of the studies in this volume, particularly those in the first section, record how much happier were the learners who engaged with a sense of mathematics as personally accessible, interpretable, applicable than with an inert body of knowledge and skills. Under these conditions, the 'language' of mathematics can be seen as reflecting personal choice as to how that piece of mathematics can be represented, developed and interrogated. Finding communalities between one piece of mathematics and another, or between one person's presentation and another, can then become part of the excitement of deriving the generalities that underpin a number of examples. Finding the deviant particular examples can lead to opening a new set of questions, which lead in a diverging direction.

But a curriculum does not only comprise the content of mathematics, the syllabus, but also the interpretation of that syllabus through the materials and resources used as well as the pedagogical style invoked to define the learning experiences. Thus, the learning outcomes from meeting Pythagoras' theorem worked on the blackboard by a teacher and followed by the students attempting a set of practice examples will not be the same as those when a group of students are invited to consider the geometric conditions under which $a^2 = b^2 + c^2$ is or is not a true statement for a triangle ABC. These are only two possible presentations. We could investigate outcomes from many others. The attained curriculum in each case, and for each student, will be different.

Heleen Verhage, a curriculum developer in The Netherlands, explores the use of contexts in the presentation and learning of mathematics. She provokes many important and unresolved questions. For example, is the use of contexts derived from women's traditional domains emancipatory or confirmatory? What impact does the deliberate choice of non-male contexts have on the learning of mathematics by all? Should bias in context choice be controlled or assessed and how? By drawing out the differences between the 'static' view of mathematics as abstract, objective, well-defined and certain and the 'dynamic' image which is creative, relative and personal, she justifies the inclusion of the latter, if for no other reason, than:

> because we believe that what I call here the dynamic image of mathematics will particularly appeal to women.

Mary Barnes and Mary Coupland take a similar approach but with a content area, calculus, acknowledged as 'difficult', and normally considered 'abstract', 'unbiased' and where any practical applications are usually in the context of projectiles. Taking an approach to curriculum development which is long overdue, and providing a model for the future, they planned a course that would help students:

to see calculus as a human creation, developed in a particular cultural and historical context, by mathematicians who were influenced by the needs and values of the society they lived in.

Again taking a positive perspective, but this time with adult women returning to study as their target group, Beth Marr and Sue Helme describe the steps they took in devising their course, and their reasons for choosing both content and method. Further education courses in mathematics have been amongst the slowest to be affected by changes in mathematics pedagogy. Innovations are long overdue and they are speaking for everyone when they write:

> We have developed what we believe are important criteria for the successful teaching—and learning—of mathematics . . . Most of these criteria apply to the teaching of mathematics to anyone . . . but are specially relevant to adult women returning to study.

For many researchers, establishing the 'current state' with respect to gender distribution and achievement is a first step in identifying issues and research questions. The third section, Gender and Achievement, begins with a chapter by Gila Hanna, Erika Kündiger and Christine Larouche, which offers an overview of sex differences relative to aspects of mathematics achievement of students in the final year of secondary school in 15 countries. The data derive from the Second International Mathematics Study. The sample of respondents was extremely large, enabling the authors to draw precise and particular conclusions about those aspects of the teaching and learning of mathematics addressed in the achievement tests taken by students, the questionnaire on student attitudes and the questionnaire completed by the teachers. This extensive quantitative study establishes that between-country gender differences are often greater than within-country differences and that any sex differences that do exist, are not consistent across all the participating countries. Gila Hanna and her colleagues discuss their findings in the light of responses to the questions about learning experiences or expectations, which have often been conjectured as explanations for differences in achievement. What they cannot do is query these responses, nor indeed the reactions to the multichoice question format of the achievement tests. It remains for qualitative studies, on a smaller scale, to probe those issues.

Berinderjeet Kaur looked at achievement within her own national boundaries of Singapore by examining the performances of girls and boys, matched in ability, in one particular mathematics syllabus taken at 16 plus and comparing their mathematics results with their results in some other subjects. Her results are consistent with those in other societies in that they demonstrate males outperforming females in general, and, in particular, in quantification and spatial visualization. By cross-comparing performance in mathematics, with performance in other subjects she challenges one frequent assertion that studying mathematics-related subjects helps performance in Mathematics. The results of Berinderjeet's girls in Mathematics correlated highly significantly with their results in Chemistry and Physics combined, Chemistry and Biology combined, English Language, Geography and Bible Knowledge. The Mathematics results of the boys in the sample, on the other hand, correlated highly significantly with their results in all of the sciences, combined and single disciplines, *except* Chemistry and Biology combined and Biology as a single subject, as well as with

English Language, English Literature and Geography. This raises interesting questions of which the relationship between Mathematics and Biology is one example. For the girls, achievement in Biology was closely related to achievement in Mathematics, but this was not so for the boys. This challenges conventional achievement analyses demonstrating very clearly how data relating to one aspect of education, in this case achievement, cannot be dissociated from all the other aspects that affect the learner's experiences. The genderization of the sciences, Biology being perceived as the 'female' science and Physics as the 'male' begs a multitude of questions about the curricula, styles of teaching and learning, social expectations, etc., which create the conditions for learning.

The final chapter in this section addresses a few of these issues in a very small-scale study in three Greek primary schools. Evangelie Tressou-Milonas looked at children's attitudes to and progress in mathematics under conditions innovatory in Greece, but widespread in the United Kingdom, that is an individualized learning scheme, in this case Scottish Mathematics Primary (SMP). She chose three schools which differed in their social class intake and her results reinforce those obtained elsewhere with respect to this age group (7 +). In both performance and attitudes girls were equal, or superior, to boys but social class was a more noticeable discriminator between pupils than was gender.

The final section of the book, Women's Presence, gathers together differing approaches to the question of the presence of women in the mathematical sciences. Joanne Becker compares the factors that influence women and men to pursue further study in computer science in two different universities in order to establish if these are similar to those identified for mathematics. Her interest is in drawing attention to strategies that institutions could adopt in order to encourage and retain women in these important areas. She underlines the attractiveness of a problem-solving methodology to those who are successful in both mathematics and computer science. This reinforces the rationale for the curriculum development ideology currently dominating both the UK and the USA which approaches school mathematics from an applicable, enquiry-based, investigational perspective.

Prue Purser and Helen Wily, on the other hand, have charted a decline in the number of all mathematics graduates in New Zealand and, in investigating the destination of mathematics graduates, draw attention to two very worrying features. First, like Joanne Becker, they found that compared with men, fewer women continue with postgraduate work thereby limiting their employment options and reinforcing the messages about the invisibility of women in mathematics-related fields. Second, mathematics graduate teachers are an endangered species. This carries dire consequences for the mathematics education of future school children. Remembering the positive responses which the Greek primary school girls made to the female mathematics researcher, the disappearance of confident, well-trained teachers of mathematics, especially females, from both primary and secondary schools removes role models as well as people sensitive to the influences upon learning of gender-related factors. This trend is not particular to New Zealand. The same phenomenon can be found in the UK and parts of the USA. At the same time, the opposite, a surfeit of trained mathematics teachers, poses different questions to educators in some parts of Europe, for example, Germany, and The Netherlands. Explanations for these trends are more likely to be found by examining the *why*

different social histories, which dictate pay, conditions of service, social status of teachers, opportunities for mathematics-related work outside of education, etc., than in differences implicit to the teaching and learning of mathematics.

The final chapter is an historical review of Italian research papers by, or about, women mathematicians over the period 1887–1946 but including some consideration of female mathematics graduates at the present time. For example, Giuseppina Fenaroli and her colleagues present interesting data comparing the percentage of women mathematics graduates in 1985 (75 per cent of 1264) with the sex of Directors of Institutes and Centres of Italian Research in 1984 (0 per cent of 7). Including mathematics amongst all science graduates reduced the percentage of women to 59.5 per cent and increased the number of directors to 151 of whom 7 were women (4 in biology and medicine). The authors consider the historical evidence about the role of women as teachers and researchers of mathematics, documenting who wrote papers, when, how many, and where these were published. They also refer to historical papers written by men about women mathematicians. Many of the social and personal issues that arise in preceding chapters are found here as explanations or conjectures about the presence of women in mathematics. Additionally, these researchers offer one model for establishing women's historical presence in the discipline. Their strategies could be of use to colleagues interested in undertaking a similar exercise in their own country.

The collection provides an international perspective on current work, original either in its focus or in its setting. In addition, it presents a breadth of approaches using both qualitative and quantitative methodologies, and, as the authors make clear, demonstrates the gains and losses to be achieved from each. It is regrettable that reports were not available from a wider selection of countries, especially those outside the British excolonial orbit, those with very different political structures and those in different stages of development. In part this is probably due to linguistic and communication constraints. In part, it is also due to the locus of development that assigns importance to researchable issues. I recall attending a seminar on mathematics and computer education in the People's Republic of China where 10 per cent of the Chinese participants were women but I was informed that gender was not an issue in Chinese mathematics education. Of the three interpreters assigned to the non-Chinese participants, two were women and both of these privately recounted experiences at school similar in content and effect to those to which I was drawing attention in the UK. The present volume provides a start in identifying trends that are replicated as well as those that appear to be contradicted and in drawing attention to the complexity of the issues pertinent to providing equal opportunities in mathematics education.

Chapter 1

Gender and Classroom Practice

Gilah C. Leder

PREFACE

Task

Draw a picture of a teacher teaching a mathematics class. Don't let lack of artistic talents impede you. Take as much time as you need to draw your picture.

Outcome

Figure 1.1. *Drawings of a mathematics teacher (by Carole and Peter, both primary school teachers).*

A number of messages are conveyed by the drawings this task produces (see, for example, Figure 1.1), the stress felt by teachers in mathematics classes among them.

INTRODUCTION

Research on classrooms has proliferated during the past three decades. Lively debate between advocates of systematic classroom observations on the one hand, and of ethnography on the other, has emphasized the difficulty of capturing and reporting the complex behaviours and interactions observed. The former, it is often argued, focuses on overt, observable behaviour at the expense of noting underlying meaningful aspects; is unable to capture the subtleties of classroom behaviours; interferes with the development of theories that recognize the complexity of that behaviour; and breaks the natural flow of interaction patterns because of its reliance on arbitrary time sampling. Developing new theoretical ideas, discovering new empirical facts, it is generally believed, is more likely to flow from work carried out within the more open-ended ethnographic framework.

> The most crucial difference between those using the prespecified coding systems and ethnographers is that the former take for granted many aspects of school life, which the ethnographer struggles to make problematic.
> (Delamont and Hamilton, 1986, p. 35)

PREVIOUS RESEARCH

A range of techniques—both qualitative and quantitative—used to monitor classroom behaviour has affirmed the importance of teacher practices and beliefs as at least a partial explanation for gender differences in educational performance and participation, particularly in the areas of mathematics and the physical sciences. For example, the extent to which gender *per se* shaped and reinforced teachers' perceptions and expectations of students was one of the themes explored by Delamont (1983) in her ethnographic study of interactions in the classroom. Walden and Walkerdine (1985) used a variety of techniques to describe and examine students' performance as they progressed from primary to secondary school. Not only did they document consistent differences in the ways teachers judged and valued the contribution of boys and girls in their mathematics classes, but they also found differences in the ways boys and girls described themselves as learners of mathematics.

Examples of students' views of mathematics, gathered in contemporary Australian primary schools, are shown in Figure 1.2. While these two examples should not be used to illustrate gender differences in attitudes to mathematics, they reveal the intensity of beliefs about mathematics shown by quite young students.

Work relying on a more quantitative systematic classroom observation approach has also revealed that teachers often interact differently with their female and male students, with males attracting more and qualitatively different interactions. Representative of research within the product-process paradigm are studies by Becker (1981), Eccles and Blumenfeld (1985), Peterson and Fennema (1985) and Stallings (1979) in American classrooms, Galton *et al.* (1980) in English classes, Dunkin and Doenau (1982) in Australian schools and Staberg (1985) in Swedish classes. Consistent, though small, differences in the classroom experiences of girls and boys are frequently reported, with the latter typically having more interactions with their teachers. Observations in high school algebra and geometry classes were summarized by Stallings (1979, p. 5) as follows:

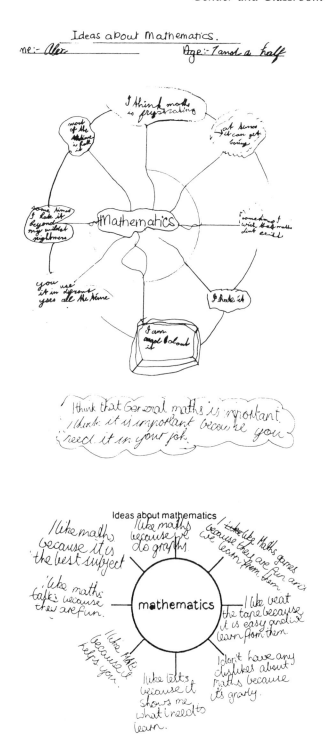

Figure 1.2. *Students' ideas about mathematics (Alex, grade 3 and Christ, grade 6).*

Though few of the differences are significant, the trend is rather clear. Men are spoken to more often than women. Men ask more questions and teachers ask men more questions. Women volunteer answers as often as do men but the men are called upon to respond more frequently than are women. Men receive a little more individual instruction and social inter-actions. Acknowledgement, praise, encouragement, and corrective feedback are given slightly more frequently to men than to women.

Since the issue of differential treatment of boys and girls by teachers has been given much prominence over more than a decade in traditional research journals, publications aimed primarily at teachers, and in the popular media, a carefully conducted study carried out in Australian classrooms seemed timely. Would monitoring of contemporary classrooms reveal a changing picture? To maximize the information obtained it seemed important to go beyond documenting frequency of interactions.

Research focusing on length of interaction, and particularly on wait time has rarely examined the impact of gender on teacher–student interactions in mathematics classes. A noteworthy exception is provided by Gore and Roumagoux (1983) who reported that grade 4 boys were given more wait time than girls in mathematics lessons. General work on wait time has indicated that the quality and scope of students' answers, and their overall achievement, tend to improve when teachers increase their wait time. Thus if boys indeed have more wait and length of interaction times than girls, this could be reflected in the quality of work produced, on average, by the two groups.

A NEW STUDY

For those engaged in contemporary research in classrooms the main purposes that motivate the work determine the most appropriate methodology to be used. Interest in detailed, qualitative analysis of patterns of social interactions makes an ethnographic approach likely to be more rewarding. However, if factual and theoretical claims are to be tested, systematic observations seem more useful. The latter approach was used in the present study, with its emphasis on reexamining interaction patterns between teachers and male and female students in their classes. Specifically, teachers' interactions with girls and boys in mathematics classes were monitored in terms of two distinct observa-tion schedules. Teacher–child dyadic interactions were quantified using an approach based on that described by Brophy and Good (1970). Length of time spent on various interactions was also monitored. The methodology used by Rowe (1974) in her 'wait-time' studies shaped the categories measured in this observation schedule.

Method

Sample

The sample, adjusted for student absences during the lessons observed, consisted of 581 students in grades 3, 6, 7 and 10: 289 boys and 292 girls. A total of 26 teachers from 14 different schools in the metropolitan area of Melbourne, Australia, participated.

Procedure

A video camera, mounted on a tripod in one corner of the room, was used to capture teacher–student interactions during mathematics lessons. Thus continuous observation of the way teachers interacted with each student in the class was possible. As well, the camera's built in stop watch allowed accurate time records to be kept. Accuracy of observations was further enhanced by using a slow tracking video replay facility.

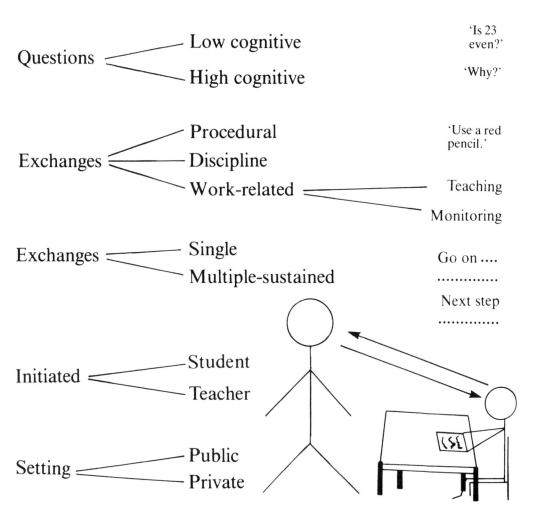

Figure 1.3. *Interaction categories recorded.*

No restrictions were placed on teachers' presentations or behaviours, apart from a request to include as much oral and questioning work as possible in the lessons to be monitored. Between two-and-a-half and three hours of lesson time were recorded for each teacher, giving a total recording time of some 70 hours. All relevant interactions that occurred between teachers and students were ultimately coded and timed.

A mathematics test was administered to each student. Teachers were also asked to rate the performance of the students in their class in terms of excellent, good, average, or below average.

Instruments

Observations schedules   Teacher–student dyadic interactions were categorized using the approach of Brophy and Good (1970) and discussed in Leder (1987a). Low and high cognitive questions addressed by the teacher to an individual student were coded, as were procedural, discipline and work-related exchanges. These last were subdivided into teaching and monitoring episodes for observations in grades 7 and 10. All student-initiated exchanges were noted. For the two higher grades, low and high cognitive level questions from students were combined into a student question category. The setting of all dyadic interactions—whether private or public—was also recorded. Figure 1.3 provides an overview of the categories recorded.

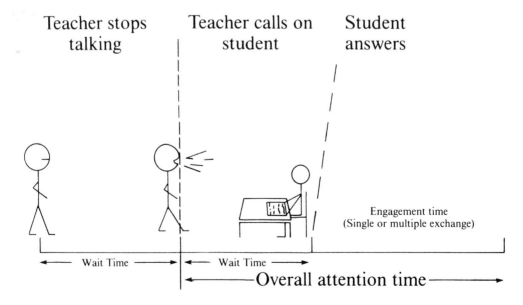

Figure 1.4.   *Time intervals observed.*

For teacher questions only, records were made of Rowe's (1974) wait time, the engagement time for subsequent single or unit exchanges, and the total attention time. Teacher attention time was defined as the time interval that begins when a student is called on plus the subsequent engagement time. Attention time between teacher and students was recorded for all interactions. Details of this scheme are summarized in Figure 1.4. Further information can also be found in Leder (1987a; 1987b).

The mathematics test   The Operations test in the Mathematics Profile Series (Australian Council for Educational Research, 1977) was administered to each student. The test consists of 20, 30, 30 and 40 items for students in grades 3, 6, 7 and 10 respectively. To allow comparisons across grade levels to be made, raw scores were converted to brytes, the unit of measurement used in the test. Each test included basic recall of fact questions as well as items that required understanding and application of underlying principles.

Results

The methodology employed, videotaping lessons in intact classes, allowed detailed, comprehensive and accurate records to be made of all teacher–student interactions for every student in the class. Repeated analysis of selected segments revealed high inter- and intra-coder reliability for each of the categories of interest.

The mathematics test

There were no statistically significant differences in the performance of boys and girls in grades 3, 6, and 7 on the mathematics test. At the grade 10 level boys achieved significantly better than girls ($t_{169} = 2.48$, $p < 0.05$).

In general, the test scores obtained coincided with the teachers' perceptions of students' ability. Students rated as excellent had the highest mean score, followed by students rated as good, then those rated as average, and finally those rated as below average. These relationships held as well when boys and girls were considered separately.

Observation schedule (1): Frequency of interactions

As can be seen from Table 1.1, in which significant differences in mean frequency of interactions with boys and girls, as well as the groups attracting more interactions, are presented, boys tended to interact more frequently than girls with their teachers, overall and for the majority of categories described.

At each of the grade levels observed boys, on average, had more interactions overall with their teachers than girls, had more discipline exchanges, more work-related exchanges, more public interactions, and more teacher-initiated interactions. Boys themselves also initiated more interactions, and publicly asked more cognitive questions. While discrepancies in mean rates of interactions with boys and girls were less

Table 1.1. *Significant differences in interactions with boys and girls.*

Interaction[†]	Grade			
	3	6	7	10
Low cognitive Q	Boys **	NS (B)	NS	NS (G)
High cognitive Q	NS (B)	NS (B)	NS	Boys ****
Procedural exchange	Boys *	NS (B)	NS (B)	Boys ***
Discipline exchange	Boys ****	Boys **	Boys ***	Boys ****
Work-related exchange	NS (B)	Boys ****	Boys **	Boys **
Students' Q			Boys **	Boys **
Total	Boys ****	Boys ****	Boys ***	Boys ****
(– discipline)[‡]	Boys *	Boys ***	Boys *	Boys ****
Setting				
Public	Boys ****	Boys **	Boys *	Boys ****
Private	NS (B)	Boys ****	Boys **	NS (B)
Initiator				
Teacher	Boys ****	Boys **	Boys *	Boys ****
Student	NS (B)	Boys ****	Boys *	Boys ****

[†] Total number of interactions monitored > 10,000.
* $p < 0.05$, ** $p < 0.01$, *** $p < 0.001$, **** $p < 0.0001$.

Note: B denotes non-significant difference in favour of Boys.

[†] Total number of interactions, other than those coded as discipline.

startling for the low and high cognitive-level questions, the consistency of non-significant findings in favour of boys is noteworthy. When all discipline exchanges were discounted boys were still found to have more interactions than girls with their teachers. The magnitude of the differences can be described as follows. For every six interactions grade 3 teachers had with the boys in their mathematics classes, they had just under five with girls. At the grade 6 level the corresponding ratios were very similar. At the grade 7 level the difference was somewhat less: the discrepancy in favour of boys was approximately 10 per cent, while at the grade 10 level for every four interactions with girls there were over five with boys.

Observation schedule (2): Time variables

The mean wait times, subsequent engagement time per unit exchange and total attention times were calculated separately for boys and girls, taking into account differences in student numbers where appropriate. Significant differences and group attracting more time are summarized in Table 1.2.

The consistent bias that characterized the data presented in Table 1.1 is not apparent in Table 1.2. Where they occurred significant differences were in terms of girls having more time in grades 3 and 10, boys in grade 6, with a mixed result in grade 7. Eight of the twelve significant findings related to the low and high cognitive question categories, with the remaining significant findings occurring for procedural exchanges (boys having more time in grade 6, girls in grade 7), discipline exchanges (boys in grade 6) and work-related exchanges (girls in grade 3).

Table 1.2. *Significant differences in times spent with boys and girls.*

Interaction	Time interval		
	Wait time	Subsequent/ time question	Attention time/exchange
Grade 3			
Low cognitive Q	Girls*	NS	NS
High cognitive Q	NS	Girls*	Girls*
Procedural exchange			NS
Discipline exchange			NS
Work-related exchange			Girls*
Grade 6			
Low cognitive Q	NS	NS	NS
High cognitive Q	NS	Boys****	Boys**
Procedural exchange			Boys*
Discipline exchange			Boys*
Work-related exchange			NS
Grade 7			
Low cognitive Q	NS	NS	NS
High cognitive Q	NS	Boys*	NS
Procedural exchange			Girls*
Discipline exchange			NS
Work-related exchange			NS
Students' Q			NS
Grade 10			
Low cognitive Q	NS	Girls****	Girls****
High cognitive Q	NS	NS	NS
Procedural exchange			NS
Discipline exchange			NS
Work-related exchange			NS
Students' Q			NS

$*p < 0.05$, $**p < 0.01$, $***p < 0.001$, $****p < 0.0001$.

DISCUSSION

Our society values mathematics. The role played by mathematics as a critical filter to further educational and career opportunities is widely recognized. Gender differences in participation and performance in post-compulsory mathematics courses have been well-documented elsewhere. Of the variety of factors frequently invoked to help explain these differences, the influence of the teacher was singled out in this chapter.

Teacher–student interactions were examined in a sample of grades 3, 6, 7 and 10 mathematics classes. Teacher influence was operationally defined in terms of frequency of interactions and time spent waiting for and interacting with students. The overall impression conveyed by the data suggests that boys and girls are treated differently in mathematics lessons.

For the majority of contacts, those initiated by teachers, boys interacted more frequently than girls with their teachers. As well, boy consistently sought and received teacher attention more frequently than girls. Yet the data with respect to time intervals spent waiting for and interacting with students were equivocal. There was no evidence of consistent teacher bias in favour of boys or girls.

It is noteworthy that the differences in teacher treatment of boys and girls reported in earlier research are still found in contemporary classrooms. The differences identified seem to precede gender differences in performance in mathematics. In this study, for example, a significant difference in the mathematics performance of boys and girls was found only at the grade 10 level. The link between teacher treatment and student achievement is suggestive, indirect, and probably further reinforced by the gender-linked expectations and beliefs of the wider society. No direct causal relationship can be deduced from the results presented. It could be argued, in fact, that the teacher behaviours quantified are symptomatic of wider social expectations and beliefs. Schools function within a cultural context, reflect it, and continue to reinforce the notion that competing in mathematics is more important for boys than for girls.

The lessons monitored in this study were generally well run by experienced and enthusiastic teachers anxious to optimize their students' learning experiences. Yet the different frequencies of interaction patterns reported several decades ago seem to persist. The similarities of the findings of this earlier research, which relied on time sampled observations of selected students, and those of the present study in which intact classes were videotaped and all relevant teacher interactions with every student for the total lesson were described, emphasizes the consistency and pervasiveness of the trends outlined. Without a similar source of data for length of time spent on interactions it is difficult to know how the time findings should be interpreted. In this study, the amount of time teachers spent with students seemed not to be affected consistently by the sex of the student (though, as reported in Leder (1987a; 1987b; 1988) perceived student ability appeared an important variable). The quite different pictures conveyed by the two observation schedules of teacher–student interactions highlight the complexity of documenting accurately and effectively the many aspects of the classroom climate.

While the data reported here sampled only a very small part of a teaching year, they allow speculations about the cumulative impact of the consistent differences, documented in this study, in teachers' behaviours towards boys and girls. It is certainly likely that they will contribute to and reinforce differences in girls' and boys' perceptions of themselves as learners of mathematics, perceptions which may ultimately be translated into differences in achievement and participation in mathematics. The relevance of mathematics to eventual life choices has already been emphasized. Contemporary treatment of boys and girls in mathematics classes still appears to place the latter at some risk.

ACKNOWLEDGEMENT

I wish to acknowledge the Australian Research Grants Scheme for the financial support of this research, and the assistance of Ingrid Leonard with the collection and analysis of the data.

REFERENCES

Becker, J. (1981) Differential treatment of females and males in mathematics classes. *Journal for Research in Mathematics Education*, **12**, 40-53.
Brophy, J.E. and Good, T.L. (1970) Teacher–child dyadic interaction: a manual for coding classroom behaviour. In Simon, A. and Boyer, E.G. (eds) *Mirrors for Behavior. An Anthology of Classroom Observation Instruments*. Philadelphia: Research for Better Schools.
Delamont, S. (1983) *Interaction in the Classroom*. London: Methuen.

Delamont, S. and Hamilton, D. (1986) Revisiting classroom research: a continuing cautionary tale. In Hammersley, M. (ed) *Controversies in Classroom Research*. Milton Keynes: Open University Press, pp. 25-43.

Dunkin, M. J. and Doenau, S. J. (1982) Ethnicity, classroom interaction and student achievement. *Australian Journal of Education*, **26**, 171-89.

Eccles, J. S. and Blumenfeld, P. (1985) Classroom experiences and student gender: are there differences and do they matter? In Wilkinson, L. C. and Marrett, C. B. (eds) *Gender Influences in Classroom Interaction*. New York: Academic Press, pp. 74-114.

Galton, M., Simon, B. and Croll, P. (1980) *Inside the Primary Classroom*. London: Routledge & Kegan Paul.

Gore, D. A. and Roumagoux, D. V. (1983) Wait time as a variable in sex related differences during fourth grade instruction. *Journal of Educational Research*, **26**, 273-5.

Leder, G. C. (1987a) Teacher student interaction: a case study. *Educational Studies in Mathematics*, **18**, 255-71.

Leder, G. C. (1987b) Student achievement: a factor in classroom dynamics? *The Exceptional Child*, **34**, 133-41.

Leder, G. C. (1988) Do teachers favour high achievers? *Gifted Child Quarterly*, **32**, 315-20.

Peterson, P. L. and Fennema, E. (1985) Effective teaching, student engagement in classroom activities, and sex-related differences in learning mathematics. *American Educational Research Journal*, **22**, 309-36.

Rowe, M. B. (1974) Wait time and rewards as instructional variables, their influence on language, logic, and fate control. Part One, Wait time. *Journal of Research in Science Teaching*, **11**, 81-94.

Staberg, E. (1985) *Girls in Science Lessons. Classroom observations in grades 3, 7 and 9*. Paper presented at the third GASAT conference, London.

Stallings, J. (1979) *Factors Influencing Women's Decisions to Enrol in Advanced Mathematics Courses: Executive Summary*. Menlo Park, CA: SRI International.

Walden, R. and Walkerdine, V. (1985) *Girls and Mathematics. From Primary to Secondary Schooling*. Bedford Way Papers 24. London: Institute of Education, University of London.

Chapter 2

'They look at you in absolute horror': Women Writing and Talking about Mathematics

Zelda Isaacson

> It's fashionable not to like maths—when you're at secondary school—they think you're weird if you like maths.
> Especially if you are a girl, yes, it's accepted for boys though, boys are supposed to be superior at maths and physics.

During the academic year 1987–88 I had the good fortune to teach mathematics to a group of women on a Hitecc (re-entry into Science and Technology) course. As well as teaching them mathematics, in the course of the year I asked the women to reflect on their experiences as learners of mathematics in the past and in the present. They recorded their views on paper, in the form of mathematical biographies, questionnaires and other written comments. I also tape-recorded and subsequently transcribed several group discussions which focused on these issues. The interchange at the head of this chapter comes from transcript material.

These were mature and thoughtful women, aged generally in their twenties and thirties, mostly well-educated in the humanities, languages or social studies, but not in science, technology or mathematics. All had made a considered choice to gain a proper education and training in the latter areas, having opted out of them at an earlier stage.

Twenty-four women joined the Polytechnic of North London's Hitecc course in September 1987, and, together with a colleague, I took on the responsibility of teaching the mathematics component. This was an interesting and challenging task. We were aware that women who had not previously chosen to study mathematics beyond the compulsory stage might have fears and anxieties which could inhibit their learning. It was therefore important to approach the work in as sensitive and supportive a way as possible. Also, it was probable that the women would bring a wide range of mathematical experience, ability and knowledge to the course, and we would have to take proper account of this. At the same time, we had to be continually aware that on this course mathematics was a service subject, and that we had to provide opportunities for all the women to become competent and confident users of mathematics in scientific and technological contexts.

We soon learned that many of the women had joined the course because their life experiences had given them confidence in their practical and technical skills—but that they were much less confident as learners of mathematics. This reinforced our conviction that the key strategies we had agreed upon were appropriate. In brief, these were: to encourage group work and discussion; to provide structured investigative activities; to legitimate the women's 'common sense' knowledge and give them confidence in their ability to learn new mathematics; and last but not least, to try to create a light-hearted classroom atmosphere where students could enjoy their work, and share experiences, activities and ideas.

Indeed, it quickly became clear that the students were enjoying our approach and that structured investigations followed by practice of skills and techniques provided a workable and effective mix of activities.

This is the practical, living context within which the women's writing and talking occurred. They wrote and talked about their past experiences, as a result of which many had become alienated from or excluded from mathematics. I also asked them to reflect on, and write about their reasons for coming on the course—this, generally, was experienced as a difficult task. Towards the end of the year, they commented on how they felt (as learners of mathematics) as a result of their experiences on the course. They also wrote about the experience of working in groups in mathematics.

What do their words tell us? How can we understand and interpret them? Can they throw light on some of the complex and little understood processes by which women come to be alienated and excluded from mathematics, science and technology—or the equally complex processes by which some women are able to be included in these domains, at one stage of their lives if not at another? Can we use comments like these as pointers to these processes?

These are crucially important questions. In most countries in the Western world, far fewer women than men study mathematics, science and technical subjects. Indeed, although more males than females study these subjects, far too few people of either sex become technologically or mathematically competent. This is increasingly a source of concern, although this concern has only manifested itself to any extent quite recently.

It is illuminating to ask for whom it is a concern and why it matters, for there are, I believe, several distinct such groups each of which has their own reasons for concern. Liberal educators, for example, believe that all people should be enabled to make real choices for self-development and self-realization. Unless there is equal access to educational goods, this ideal cannot be realized. Another group is that of feminists, some of whom see the issue in terms of individual freedoms, others in terms of power (and some both). A third perspective is provided by those who are concerned with the economic welfare of society, and fear the long-term consequences of too small a body of scientifically and mathematically literate people in the workforce. Of these groups, only feminists are concerned primarily with *female* underrepresentation in these important areas of work and knowledge. Liberal educators are equally concerned about males who lack opportunities for real choices—and economists and politicians would be perfectly content if only there were enough 'bodies' to fill the necessary jobs. They would, in general, not be bothered if all these turned out to be males!

Nonetheless, it is this third group, I believe, who have been mainly responsible for the improved press which the 'women and mathematics' and 'women and technology' issue has had recently. Their concern is merely another instance of the way in which women's labour is called upon in a variable way according to the economic demands of society. During each of the great wars this century, society discovered how useful and capable women were, although previously (and subsequently) this was denied. Nurseries were set up so that women could work in shipyards and factories in the secure knowledge that their children were being well looked after. Propaganda films of the time show contented children being looked after by trained staff, while their mothers go happily to work. As soon as the wars were over and men returned from the battlefields needing employment, the old messages returned. We were told that 'woman's place is in the home' and that children deprived of their mothers' constant attention were sure to suffer irreparable psychological damage! The so-called 'Bowlby era', after the second world war, is a particularly obvious example of this process at work. At present, we have a shortage of trained scientists, technologists, engineers and mathematicians, and so the 'solution' is to encourage women (and men who might not otherwise do so) to enter these professions and related occupations.

Although those of us who look at the question from the viewpoint of a liberal educator or from a feminist perspective should welcome this development, we should also constantly remain conscious of its roots. There is a risk of negative, as well as the hope of positive outcomes. If as a result of economic need, women are enabled to become more powerful in society, in economic and other terms, and to have greater freedom of choice, then those are positive outcomes for individual women and society as a whole. Especially, if more women are employed in scientific and technological work, there is hope of a gradual change of direction in these fields from a concentration on destruction to a concern for humanity. However, if trained women are kept in positions of low economic and political power, for example because of a lack of adequate childcare facilities, then little has been achieved. Worse, efforts to bring about deeper improvements could be impeded if many people believe that everything necessary is already being done.

It is precisely in this context, i.e. lack of trained 'manpower' that the notion of Hitecc courses was conceived. Hitecc (Higher Introductory Technology and Engineering Conversion Courses) is used to describe one-year conversion courses for people with post-16 qualifications in subjects other than mathematics and physics. In 1987/88, the course at the Polytechnic of North London was one of 26 such courses around the country—but the only one recruiting just women. To reiterate, the important thing for politicians is to have more 'bodies' for the technical jobs. A great deal of public money has gone into developing Hitecc courses, but most of this has been spent on men. Only 114 of the 473 students who enrolled in this year were women and 24 of these were on our course. Nonetheless, this is a better ratio than on physics, engineering, and other technical courses generally, and those women who did enrol on Hitecc courses were given an opportunity to acquire valuable skills and qualifications.

Both Teresa Smart (the colleague with whom I shared the mathematics teaching) and I have a particular interest in the 'girls and mathematics' issue. We are well versed in the gender and mathematics research literature, and are also both experienced secondary school mathematics teachers who have moved into teacher education. These interests and experience contributed to the theoretical framework within which we planned the mathematics course. That is, developments in the pedagogy of mathematics at school level as well as the literature on gender and mathematics and on mathematics anxiety provided our starting points. (See Bibliography.) This led us to adopt the key strategies which are described briefly above.

THE WOMEN'S WORDS

In the week prior to the start of the course, my colleague Teresa met the students at an informal lunch. She reported that, when she was introduced as 'one of the mathematics tutors', several of the women expressed their anxieties about mathematics, and especially fear of being 'shown up' in public. Typical was the comment of one woman who said 'you won't ask me questions that I can't answer *in front of the whole class*, will you?'. Another said 'I'm not telling anyone, but I'm scared!'—and someone responded 'So am I!'.

The following week, on the first day of term, I asked all the women to write their own mathematical biographies, and to describe, in particular, those memories that seemed important to them. This was followed some weeks later by group discussions which focused on issues raised in the biographies. A number of themes, some of which are by now familiar in the gender and mathematics literature, emerged. Several women wrote about the negative effects on their learning of a competitive environment. For example:

> Especially in maths I couldn't stand the competitiveness of seeing the 'clever boy' (there's always one in every class!) do the exercises miles before everyone else and understanding things quicker than everybody which just reinforced the idea that I didn't have a 'mathematical brain'.

And another woman who had studied but not taken 'A' level mathematics wrote:

> The problems came with my 'A' level maths—it was awful. Firstly I was in a class of 20 and I was the only female. I think in the 2 years I did it I hardly questioned anything about the work . . . I found everything was so competitive that to ask one of your classmates for help was a joke.

Another theme concerned fear and panic in mathematics lessons:

> At about 8 or 9 I had a totally intimidating teacher (the headmaster) for maths, for one term. He taught us times-tables in a militaristic type of way: chanting out a times-table, pointing at you and expecting you to fire back an answer within a second. If unable to answer some fate worse than death would be waiting. That is how it seemed when I was a completely powerless, timid 8-year-old. From then on started a slippery slope downhill. Although I had some good encouraging teachers along the way, I had come to associate maths with fear and panic.

In one of the group discussions, a woman described how her teacher had given her 'licks' (smacks with a ruler) if she could not answer a question. This had left her with a fear of mathematics which she was now, many years later, determined to overcome.

Yet another recurrent theme was the way teachers either did not encourage, or even actively discouraged, girls from doing mathematics—often rationalizing this by saying that the student was better at other subjects. For example:

> The maths teacher had 12 pupils, 5 of whom were girls. I do not know how exaggerated my memory has become, but I do remember him saying that girls had no place in his field. By the end of the term, there were only two of us girls left and he did make life hard for us. In the end I dropped maths and was told not to worry, because my aptitude lay in languages anyway.

Another perspective on this is provided by the woman who said:

> I wish my teacher had told me I was capable of doing maths a lot earlier than she had . . .

Yet another woman commented (in discussion) that it had never occurred to her that she might study mathematics beyond 'O' level (although she was quite good at it) because she was 'better' at English and History. I asked her whether anyone at school or home had suggested she consider going on with maths, but she said no one had ever done so. This conversation took place *after* this student had completed her questionnaire, where she wrote that her feelings about herself as a learner of mathematics before joining the course were 'not terribly positive' and that she felt that way because 'I wasn't very good at it at school'. In other words, her immediate response had been that she hadn't been 'good at maths' and therefore hadn't felt positive about it, yet when exploring this more fully she realized that she had been quite capable of doing maths at school—but had been 'better at' other subjects. When teased out, being 'better at' other subjects turned out to mean getting better marks for, and enjoying more, these other subjects.

Several women made comments which, explicitly or implicitly, point to the significance of the image of mathematics. One very explicitly said:

> I think it's got something to do with an image, to do with prestige, because mathematical concepts are more difficult and considered to be more difficult to understand than factual statements about sequences in history . . .

Other comments, like the words which head this paper ('. . . they think you're weird if you like maths . . .') indicated the importance of the image of mathematics in other ways. The woman who had said this also neatly encapsulated both peer group influence and the image of mathematics in one statement:

> . . . like at work—I work at a restaurant at the weekend, and everybody else is either a student or an artist . . . everybody else is sort of arty, and they say—what are you studying—and I say, physics, chemistry and maths—they look at you in absolute horror, and that's the end of the conversation, because they can't think of another thing to say . . .

Family pressures are another important influence. One woman said:

> Well, when I told my mother about going on this course now, she thinks I've totally flipped—she can't understand it—well, what kind of jobs are you going to get, you know—are you going to be a motor mechanic, or something . . . it's really funny . . . you know, if I'd said to her, oh, I'm doing an evening class in philosophy, or something, she'd say, oh, how wonderful . . . you know . . .

And another woman described the attitude of her father-in-law, who had been a chemist all his life. She said that:

> . . . (he) thinks it's funny, he thinks it's absolutely hilarious that I'm doing this . . . he can't understand why I'm doing it—I'm married, got a husband, got a family, why do I need to . . . like, if I want to work, I could go and work, why do I want to be doing this? . . .

This last comment resonates with what I believe is one of the most influential and deeply rooted processes by which girls and women are excluded from 'male' activities. In other papers I have described what I call a 'coercive inducement'—an inducement which is so powerful that it comes to act as a coercion. (See, for example, Isaacson, 1986, pp. 223-40; Isaacson, 1989.) A picture is painted for women of the wonderful, rewarding world of love, marriage, children, home—a world which no woman in her right mind would want to reject in order to compete with men in their own world. Isadora, the central character in Erica Jong's *Parachutes and Kisses* (1984) sums it up in these words:

> Think what flak she could have avoided by being her grandfather's good granddaughter rather than the bad girl of American letters! Think of all the attacks she could have avoided, all the grief she would never have known, all the uncertainties she would have sidestepped, all the empty pages she would never have faced! And think of the garlands of praise she would have garnered, the pontifical pats on the back, the approving nods, the loving looks. No woman born in this world is immune to the pleasures of being good.
>
> (pp. 53-4)

However, an additional, possibly more positive, perspective also emerged from the women's words. This is the notion that girls do not necessarily opt out of mathematics and science because of negative reasons. They also, for good reasons, opt into other areas of study. Sometimes this is because of imaginative and inspiring teaching:

> . . . I had two English teachers who were absolutely brilliant . . . and did a lot of extra-curriculum work . . . it makes it feel as if liberal arts teachers have got a personal interest in the work their students are doing . . . and enthusiasm for their subject and that's what made it seem to me that maths didn't have the potential for sparking the imagination and being fun. It was only English that was presented that way—and languages as well.

Another commented:

> I had a couple of really good teachers at my school, you were always sorry when the lesson ended—unfortunately, it wasn't maths . . .

And a third said that she thought that girls had more imagination than boys—and hence were more likely to be attracted to subjects where they thought they could use this ability. None of the women had had any experiences while at school which suggested to them that mathematics or science were areas where imagination or creative ability could be used. Instead, the way mathematics was often experienced is summed up in the following interchange between two of the women:

> Well, they just kind of came along and gave you various sets of rules, didn't they? That's how I was taught, anyway.
>
> And little books to look them up in.
>
> Yeah, there's your rules, off you go and use them . . .
>
> If you've got something, and you don't know what you're ever going to use it for, you don't bother learning it.
>
> That's right.

Yet another theme to emerge was concerned with school organization, for example with regard to option choices, and the expectations that schools conveyed to girls. Several women described how sciences had been set against subjects like sociology or literature, which girls were expected to do. One said:

> I just think it's really funny that in my class—I can't remember any of the women going on to take 'A' level sciences at all. They were all put into Arts subjects—like you must go and do Sociology.

She continued:

> People came along and gave us various talks about what careers you could go off and do, but none of them involved science apparently—it's very strange.

These women's words underline the complexity of the processes by which girls and women come to be, at times, alienated and excluded from mathematics and at other times enabled to participate. Each of the women had her reason or reasons for having opted out earlier. There were common themes, but within this, each turned out to have had a unique package of past experiences, which had culminated in the same result—not learning sciences and mathematics although being perfectly capable of doing so. We can learn a great deal that is of relevance for classroom, school and general educational practice from these women's words. We have to admit, though, that some of the influences on girls and women, probably the most significant influences, are outside the control of teachers and schools. We can help, and can certainly improve matters, but we cannot, on our own, achieve a radical alteration of the powerful messages which girls receive from so many quarters. We have to work within these constraints and must take account of them if we are to be even partially effective. This realization makes it even more imperative to take every possible action, in our own schools and classrooms, which will minimize girls' drift away from mathematics, science and technology.

IMPLICATIONS FOR CLASSROOM PRACTICE

What can we tease out from these women's writing and talking that is relevant to classroom practice? Clearly, the attitude of teachers is of great importance. Girls need to be told that they are capable of doing mathematics—even if to the teacher this seems obvious. They need to be made aware of the many potential uses of mathematics in their own lives. And girls' career options need to be opened up so as to include many traditionally male areas of work where mathematics is needed—science, banking and insurance, technology, engineering, etc. In particular, the potential contribution of these fields to human welfare needs to be emphasized.

Mathematics classrooms need to become places where originality, independent and creative thinking and imagination are valued. Individuals' contributions and ideas must be welcomed, not rejected. Common-sense knowledge should be validated and built upon, rather than relegated to the category of irrelevant and unimportant knowledge. All this implies using an investigative open-ended approach whenever possible—and it is possible more often than teachers generally acknowledge. Mathematics classrooms should also be places where pupils come to have fun and to be intellectually stimulated (in the way literature classrooms often are) rather than to be filled with rules. These measures would improve mathematics classrooms for all pupils, but especially for girls.

Fear and anxiety are wholly negative, damaging emotions that should have no place in mathematics classrooms. Teachers need to be fully aware of how easy it is to engender these feelings—and how important it is, instead, to strive to create a relaxed, supportive, non-competitive environment where pupils can gain and maintain confidence in their mathematical abilities.

And last, but not least, mathematics classrooms need to be places where talk is encouraged and where collaborative, co-operative work is the norm. The effect on the women of working in groups was more dramatic than anything else in the year, as these comments, all written at the end of a lesson, indicate:

> It was useful because we could argue until we all agreed (or agreed to disagree) on a point. As we are teaching each other we all get a better understanding of the subject matter.

> It was nice being able to share ideas. The group members were helpful to each other which made the activities easier to tackle.

> Working in a group today has been enjoyable. Three people actively participated and the other two women although not so vocal were working through the exercises and following the arguments and discussion. The group was lively and I felt I was thinking about what I was doing and being encouraged to participate when otherwise I would have day dreamed or felt stuck.

> I find that working in groups helps mathematical ideas to develop and be maintained, since discussion encourages a deeper understanding of the subject. Group work also inspires confidence, and enables the time to pass quickly and pleasantly.

And in one of the tape-recorded discussions, a woman described her previous experiences of learning mathematics as 'a nightmare—quite horrendous' and then continued:

> . . . the way we're being taught now, is, . . . I'm really enjoying it—it's so much fun—. . . working in groups, just in groups—I've never ever worked in groups in maths before—it's really, it's really eye opening . . .

It seems appropriate to end this paper on a note of optimism. The woman referred to earlier, who had 'not terribly positive' feelings about herself as a learner of mathematics when she joined the course, wrote that as a result of her experiences on the course her feelings were now:

> . . . positive. I enjoy maths and look forward to continuing with the subject on a chemistry degree. I have also found myself 'selling' it to friends and relatives.

Working with and talking with the women on the Hitecc course was a challenging, pleasurable and rewarding experience. I thank them all for their friendship and their words.

BIBLIOGRAPHY

Burton, L. (ed.) (1986) *Girls into Maths Can Go.* London: Holt, Rinehart & Winston.
Buxton, L. (1981) *Do You Panic about Mathematics?* London: Heinemann Education.
Chipman, S. F., Brush, L. R. and Wilson, D. M. (eds) (1985) *Women and Mathematics: Balancing the Equation.* Hillsdale, NJ: Lawrence Erlbaum.
Harding, J. (ed.) (1986) *Perspectives on Gender and Science.* London: Falmer Press.
Isaacson, Z. (1986) Freedom and girls' education: a philosophical discussion with particular reference to mathematics. In Burton, L. (ed.) *Girls into Maths Can Go.* London: Holt, Rinehart & Winston.
Isaacson, Z. (1987) *Teaching GCSE Mathematics.* London: Hodder & Stoughton.
Isaacson, Z. (1989) Of course you *could* be an engineer, dear, but wouldn't you *rather* be a nurse or teacher or secretary? In Ernest, P. (ed.) *Mathematics Teaching: The State of the Art.* London: Falmer Press.
Jong, E. (1984) *Parachutes and Kisses.* London: Panther.
Kelly, A. (ed.) (1987) *Science for Girls?* Milton Keynes: Open University Press.
Royal Society (1986) *Girls and Mathematics* (A report by the Joint Mathematical Education Committee of the Royal Society and the Institute of Mathematics and Its Applications). London: The Royal Society.
Russell, S. (1983) *Factors Influencing the Choice of Advanced Level Mathematics by Boys and Girls.* Centre for Studies in Science Education, University of Leeds
Smith, S. (1987) *Separate Beginnings?* Manchester: Equal Opportunities Commission.
Walden, R. and Walkerdine, V. (1985) *Girls and Mathematics: From Primary to Secondary Schooling* (Bedford Way Paper 24). London: Institute of Education.

Chapter 3

Mathematics: Pleasure or Pain?

Máire Rodgers

Statistics show that not only do girls drop out of mathematics in greater numbers than boys when that choice becomes available, but that only a very small percentage of *all* students, male or female, take the subject at higher levels. Now if it could be argued that the majority who drop out of mathematics do not need to continue their study of the subject, then their disappearance from the field may not actually matter very much. If they have experienced undistressed learning they will have achieved a certain level of mathematical competence and also a confidence in their ability to learn. This leaves the way open for them to re-engage with mathematics at some later date if that seems either necessary or desirable to them. However, the evidence is that enormous numbers of people end up with 'feelings of anxiety, helplessness, fear and even guilt' about mathematics (Cockcroft, 1982), and for too many it remains 'a subject to be endured, not enjoyed, and to be dropped as soon as the necessary examination results have been achieved' (Skemp, 1971). No doubt, some mathematics learning has taken place, but this kind of distressed learning makes it very difficult, if not impossible, for the learner to expand her/his experience of mathematics at a later date without the help of some remedial or recovery process.

The notion that mathematics learning should be a pleasurable activity is a recurring theme in statements of the 'aims' of mathematics education as put forward by government agencies and teaching bodies in Britain during this century (McNelis and Dunn, 1977). However, as the Cockcroft Report (1982) and other studies (e.g. Buxton, 1981) indicate, the widespread prevalence of 'maths anxiety' among the general population shows that this aim has been largely unrealized in practice. Whether or not 'the pleasure principle' should be regarded as a prime purpose of studying mathematics, there is evidence to suggest that enjoyment is an essential element in the learning process. It seems that for undistressed learning to take place the learning situation must be sufficiently enjoyable to enable the learner to persist through the difficulties and frustrations that are an inevitable part of any learning experience and the learner must be feeling good about her/himself. This may appear to be so obvious as to be almost trivial, yet in practice it seems to be incredibly difficult to achieve.

A CASE STUDY

Leone Burton (1987) has written about the common stereotypical image of mathematics as a 'hard' subject. In a recent case study (Rodgers and Mahon, 1987) which tried to identify some of the factors that had encouraged female students in three Northern Ireland schools to study Advanced level ('A' level) mathematics in the sixth form, this popular view of mathematics as a 'hard' subject was referred to by about a third of the females interviewed. Some had come to the conclusion that this myth had made mathematics 'a hundred times more difficult' and they said things like:

> If we hadn't been told this we could have gone in with a more open mind.

Nonetheless, the most common reason given by both girls and boys for choosing mathematics was because they 'liked it'. For some this was primarily because they felt they were good at it. The enjoyment came as a result of the success they had experienced. For others it had to do with the pleasure derived from the mathematics itself, like that of 'fiddling around with numbers' or the mental challenge of solving a problem. For some the pleasure was in arriving at the answer. For others it was more in the process of getting there. Others referred to the logical nature of mathematics and the satisfaction of being able to rely on their own conclusions.

Teachers

The other most important factor which many of the students regarded as influential in their choice was the encouragement, support or enthusiasm of particular teachers. The most enjoyable learning took place in an atmosphere that was light, lively and purposeful. It was clear that the individual personality and style of each teacher played a unique role in the students' experience of mathematics and the mathematics classroom.

Many of the girls were able to recall specific incidences when the clearly communicated message from a teacher or parent that they were good at mathematics enabled them to overcome some hurdle. The persistence of one teacher who was not put off by one girl's underestimation of herself was cheerfully acknowledged:

> She has encouraged me all the way along. I wasn't going to carry on. It took her three quarters of an hour solid talking to convince me that I could do it. She would like to see me lose my inferiority complex towards maths . . . No matter how bad it is going I don't regret having taken it and kept it on. It is the feeling of getting the answer right at the end of the question!

That the teacher's high expectation of the student's success facilitates learning and that the reverse, perceived underestimation, can hinder learning, was exemplified by another girl when comparing her experience with two teachers in school and one outside school to whom she had gone for extra tuition. With one teacher she had enjoyed the subject, found the teacher 'easy to understand', and had been achieving grade 'A'. This teacher left the school and she had felt that the new teacher's low expectations of her had affected her performance:

She didn't seem to think I was very good at maths so I didn't work very much at it. With the first teacher she seemed to think I was better at it and I had less difficulty with her.

Unknown to the new teacher she had got extra tuition for a month outside school and she attributed her success at 'O' level to her tutor's belief in her:

I worked very well with him because he would say my maths was good. He encouraged me.

This girl was very annoyed at the surprise her school teacher had shown when she heard her results and at seeing her in the additional mathematics class:

I don't think she actually disliked me but I don't think she thought I was going to do particularly well at additional, which I didn't.

Although she attributed her failure in additional mathematics to difficulty with the mechanics section of the course, her attitude, enjoyment and commitment to the subject had obviously suffered as a result of her perception of the teacher's opinion of her potential.

There was plenty of evidence to suggest that sometimes a word of encouragement, or the perception that a teacher or parent believed in her ability to succeed, was all that was necessary to enable a girl to persevere and to push through a difficult patch. But at other times all the validation in the world could not compensate for the failure to diagnose precisely where a student's difficulty lay with a particular bit of mathematics learning and to intervene accordingly.

One girl who had chosen not to do 'A' level reported having had difficulty with the mechanics section of the additional mathematics course. She felt frustrated by her inability to do it despite the fact that she 'kept on trying' and neither she nor her teacher ever got to the root of the problem:

She was saying not to worry, she was being confident for me . . . She kept saying to work at it, but I still couldn't do it.

It is a common finding that girls are more likely to attribute their success to hard work or luck rather than to their ability. The general consensus of the teachers we interviewed was that they usually found the girls at the upper end of the school 'very industrious'. So a girl who was already doing the best she could was being exhorted to 'try again' or 'work harder' with the implication that this would solve the problem. When she still did not succeed she concluded that she must not have worked hard enough or that she was basically unable to do it. In either case it appeared that she had taken the responsibility for her failure on herself and another layer of confidence was presumably internally eroded.

Likes and dislikes

It was in the reasons they gave for liking or disliking particular parts of the course that the most striking difference between the responses of the girls and boys appeared.

Only one of the girls doing 'A' level preferred mechanics to pure mathematics. She said:

> It is more physical and you can see the problem whereas in pure maths it is just working things out. Mechanics is like working out a real problem.

Most of the others preferred pure mathematics, typical reasons given being that it was:

> more straightforward and easy to understand

or:

> In pure maths you know exactly what you've got to do to get a certain answer.

About a third of the girls doing 'A' level mathematics and most of those who had not chosen it said that they did not like the mechanics part of the course, the main reason proffered being the difficulty of knowing how to tackle the problem.

> If you don't get the diagram right then you get the question wrong. If the questions are worded awkwardly then it's hard to draw the diagram.

> You can be wrong right from the very beginning in mechanics.

At first glance it looked as if in general the girls preferred pure mathematics to mechanics, but two of those who had not chosen 'A' level gave exactly the same reasons for preferring mechanics to pure mathematics as the above girls did for the reverse.

> The mechanics was more straightforward. Pure maths, if you got the first part wrong then maybe you'd get the complete question wrong.

> Statistics and mechanics are OK because if you learn the formulas with these areas then you can apply them.

Another girl who had dropped out of the further mathematics class had done so for the same reason:

> One reason I dropped further maths was because when I am shown a method I can follow it and I can use it in other questions. In further maths I would find it difficult to look at things and know where to start.

In contrast, both the content and the reasons for liking or disliking parts of the course were different for the boys. About half of them preferred mechanics mainly because:

> It is more related to physical things.

or:

> In the mechanics you can visualize and see what is going on.

A common reason given by the boys for preferring a particular part of the course was that it had more variety and was more interesting than another part. The reasons given for not liking a part of the course were not about it being more difficult, as was the case for the girls, but rather about it being 'boring'. Pure mathematics, especially trigonometry, was seen by some as having 'too much to learn' in the way of equations or formulae, whereas:

In mechanics if you had a mathematical mind then you could work them out.

The two boys who disliked mechanics did so for the same reason as others disliked pure maths:

> In pure maths you've got to think about it a bit more, you have got to use more things that you know . . . I think if you are doing mechanics you are using the formula over and over again.
>
> In mechanics there is a set method and you have to follow steps which can be boring.

So to summarize, it appeared that girls preferred what they considered to be more straightforward types of problems where they could follow recognized procedures and had most difficulty where the initial formulation of the problem was not so obvious to them. Boys preferred problems in which they encountered variety and which they found easy to visualize and disliked what they considered to be boring and repetitious. The fact that for girls their likes happened more often to be in pure mathematics and for boys in mechanics seemed to be secondary.

Learning styles

This appears to concur with Rosalinde Scott-Hodgetts' (1986) suggestion that early experiences and the predominant style of primary school teaching predisposes girls to develop a step by step serialized style of learning to the neglect of a more versatile style. Then, in secondary school when they are faced with the necessity of using a more holistic or exploratory approach, they find themselves at a loss. Our study seemed to indicate that even for the girls who had made it into 'A' level mathematics, there seemed still to be a heavy reliance on the serialist approach. The view of one mathematics teacher interviewed was similar to that expressed by two others:

> I think girls tend to be more at home with a routine. They like to learn a trick and go off and do tricks like that with other problems. They don't like to be put in the situation where they don't know what is going to happen to them before they start. They have this fear that maybe it won't occur to them what to do at all . . . They would be more inclined to go home and worry about it.

While this comment does in some ways accord with the girls' avowed preferences it has to be asked to what extent it is part of a self-fulfilling prophecy. To what extent are girls cossetted and allowed to remain unchallenged by mathematical situations which require more flexibility of approach for their solution rather than sets of predictable procedures?

NEW TEACHING STYLES

The new GCSE programmes in the UK hold out the possibility of providing such challenges, with their emphases on investigative methods, open-ended problems and mathematics relevant to 'real life'. However, it has to be remembered that new syllabuses of themselves are no guarantee that either teaching or learning will be any different. As Leone Burton (1987) has pointed out, a fundamental change in pedagogy is essential if the real world of mathematics and mathematical processes is to be made available to more students.

Having said this, let us not underestimate the difficulty of the task. In a previous study in one of the schools in our sample (Roberts, 1984), a teacher who was investigating the mathematical difficulties of a group of low-achieving fourth year girls found that investigations and problem-solving were greatly disliked, even when she tried to make it 'fun' or when she produced materials which she thought would interest the girls. They seemed to find it 'too scary all together' not having a recognizable framework within which to work. In her opinion, with respect to the students' experience in secondary school, the first two years are crucial in terms of establishing a girl's confidence in her ability to learn mathematics. She said:

If you lose them then, you've lost them.

This was borne out for us in our study of the 'A' level students. Very few students reported consistently good experience in mathematics classes, but about half of the boys and slightly less than half of the girls remembered almost always liking it, being good at it or of having had a series of what they considered to be 'good teachers'. The rest remembered particular turning points when it suddenly became easier or more interesting. For some this happened in the late years of primary school, for others it happened within the first three years of secondary school, almost always with a change of teacher.

Now presumably if children experienced the kind of mathematical pedagogy that Leone Burton is advocating, right from the beginning, many of the barriers to majority enjoyment and participation in mathematics might be removed. In particular, the move towards collaborative group work and language-intensive processes might benefit girls. However, in the interim period, girls who have been taught to be comfortable only with straightforward types of problems where they can use known routines and where the emphasis is on closure and correctness, are plunged into open-ended situations which require a higher level of risk-taking and uncertainty than any of our students, male or female, have hitherto encountered in the mathematics classroom. Unless account is taken of the effect of girls' previous experience (and areas of success) in mathematics, the current move towards 'problem-solving and real-life mathematics' may leave girls in a situation where the last state is worse than the first.

FAMILY MATHS

One of the initiatives that has tried to provide safe environments for young people to encounter such risky mathematical situations is the Family Math programs developed at the Lawrence Hall of Science, University of California, Berkeley. In the spring of 1987 I taught a six-week experimental class at the University of Ulster at Coleraine which was modelled on the Lawrence Hall program. The purpose was to provide an opportunity for parents and young people to do some interesting, challenging mathematics together. It was advertised as an extramural course of the university and parents were invited to attend with their 9–12-year-olds so the participants were self-selected. Of the seven families who took part in the class there were three mother–daughter pairs, two father–daughter, one mother–son and one father–son. On some days when one parent could not attend the young person usually persuaded the other parent or, in one case, an adult family friend to come along.

The emphasis was on practical problem-solving and investigational activities, with follow-up suggestions for further exploration at home. At each workshop three or four short starting puzzles were presented which could be worked on as people arrived. The main part of the class was given to another two or three activities, usually unrelated. A hand-out summarized what had been covered and contained further ideas for follow-up work. At the end of each class the participants were asked to fill out comment cards with evaluation, suggestions and questions.

Several strands ran through each workshop. In terms of what might conventionally be called the 'mathematical content' these included:

- number work (games using small numbers, calculators, mental arithmetic);
- spatial activities (using two- and three-dimensional materials, using visual imagination);
- developing strategies for problem-solving (e.g. in a version of the ancient Chinese game of Nim);
- detecting patterns, making and testing hypotheses (e.g. spirolaterals).

The atmosphere in the class was deliberately kept light and lively, with a large element of play incorporated into the proceedings. This was not to say that the work was not taken seriously. The agenda for each class also paid specific attention to issues such as:

- teaching each other to solve problems without telling the answer;
- co-operative working;
- talking about the work in progress;
- expressing feelings of delight, exuberance or frustration arising from the activities of the class;
- having fun!

In the comments received at the end of each class both young people and adults frequently mentioned that they found particular puzzles or activities 'hard'. But in contrast to the 'A' level students in the previous study, the Family Maths class almost always coupled 'hard' with 'enjoyable'. Typical comments were as follows:

> Mum liked the sticks because it was hard to work out. I liked the puzzle because it looked very easy but it wasn't.
> (For these activities see Downie *et al.*, 1981, p. 67 and Stenmark *et al.*, 1986, p. 187)

> I think it was good. The tangrams were very hard. The math maps is hard but I loved it.
> (See SMILE poster 0778 and Kaseberg *et al.*, 1980, p. 80).

> Classic fun! Plus I was brilliant at all the games which were hard. The easy ones I was not good at!

In the whole six weeks only one girl reported being bored with one activity which she found too repetitive. All the other feedback was that the classes were fun, that the work was interesting, and that it made people 'really think'. Comments from the parents indicated that the young people appeared to be more confident, not only about mathematics, but also about their general school work.

AN ENJOYABLE LEARNING ENVIRONMENT

Now obviously there are many differences between the classes the 'A' level students had experienced and this rather specialized type of Family Maths class. Not least are the facts that the latter took place outside school hours, outside school premises, that the participants were there by choice, and that nothing resembling school assessment procedures was involved. Quite apart from all other issues, however, I want to highlight three aspects of the Family Maths class which seemed to be specific contributors to the learning environment being an enjoyable one.

First is the fact that the adults and young people came to the class as peer learners. Quite often the young people were able to solve a problem before the parent and it gave them great satisfaction to assume the role of teacher. The second point, which I want to take alongside the first, has already been mentioned. It is that a lot of the enjoyment in the class stemmed from the fact that the work was 'hard'.

There is a fine line between on the one hand, putting the kind of undue pressure on young people which generates anxiety and fear about mathematics, and on the other hand, underestimating their potential and making the mathematics so easy for them that they become bored through lack of challenge and imagination. In either case blocks can be created which prevent good learning taking place. The fine line between these two extremes which enables the learner to flourish seems to require a combination of relaxed high expectation of their success, lots of encouragement and believable validation and the respect for their intelligence which recognizes that in many situations it is the learner who is the expert. Along with this, it seems that the learning situation must contain a fine balance of *sufficient* challenge and *sufficient* experience of success. Too much or too little of either can produce anxiety and mental paralysis or boredom and apathy.

The final point has to do with the use of humour, laughter and play. The Cockcroft Report emphasizes the importance of talk as something that facilitates thinking in the mathematics classroom. I should like to add to this the important role that laughter seems to have in clarifying the learner's thinking. All the evidence points to the fact that the use of humour and laughter are very useful in dissipating the tensions created by learning difficulties and which, unless they are relieved in some fashion, soak up so much of the student's attention as to create learning blocks. Also, if there is an element of play involved, then people can tackle sophisticated skills and concepts which, if they are presented in another context, will seem to be very difficult. As programs such as Family Math indicate, it is possible to take mathematics seriously, but not at all solemnly, and to change the experience of mathematics learning to one in which pleasure vastly outweighs pain.

NOTE

Part of this paper is taken from the report of a case study by Rodgers and Mahon (1987). The data in this study were mainly collected by means of semistructured interviews conducted with 45 pupils selected from three schools. The principals, careers teachers and a selection of mathematics teachers from two of the schools were also interviewed. Along with this, relevant information about the school structures and policies, and statistical information about the individual students was collected.

The sample of 45 students comprised all girls in the three schools who were in 'A' level mathematics classes (21), and for comparison 12 boys who were in the 'A' level mathematics classes and 12 girls who had done well at Ordinary level ('O' level) mathematics but who had not taken it on to 'A' level.

REFERENCES

Burton, L. (ed.) (1986) *Girls into Maths Can Go*. London: Holt, Rinehart & Wilson.

Burton, L. (1987) Women and mathematics: is there an intersection? *IOWME Newletter*, **3**(1).

Buxton, L. (1981) *Do You Panic About Maths?* London: Heinemann.

Cockcroft, W. H. (Chair) (1982) *Mathematics Counts* (Report of the Committee of Inquiry into the Teaching of Mathematics in Schools in England and Wales). London: HMSO.

Downie, D., Slesnick, T. and Stenmark, J. K. (1981) *Math for Girls and Other Problem Solvers*. Berkeley, CA: Lawrence Hall of Science, University of California.

Kaseberg, A., Kreinberg, N. and Downie, D. (1980) *Use Equals to Promote the Participation of Women in Mathematics*. Berkeley, CA: Lawrence Hall of Science, University of California.

McNelis, S. and Dunn, S. (1977) Why teach mathematics? *International Journal of Mathematical Education in Science and Technology*, **8**(2), 175-184.

Roberts, S. M. (1984) *The Study of Some Female Secondary School Underachievers in Mathematics*. MA Thesis. Coleraine: The New University of Ulster.

Rodgers, M. and Mahon, M. (1987) Opting in: girls' choice of A-level mathematics—a case study. *CORE* (Collected Original Resources in Education) **11**(3).

Scott-Hodgetts, R. (1986) Girls and mathematics, the negative implications of success, in Burton, L. (ed.) *Girls into Maths Can Go*. London: Holt, Rinehart & Wilson.

Skemp, R. R. (1971) *The Psychology of Learning Mathematics*. Harmondsworth: Penguin.

SMILE: Poster 0778 (1982) Illustration S. Cardy: Mathematical Association.

Stenmark, J. K., Thompson, V. and Cossey, R. (1986) *Family Math*. Berkeley, CA: Lawrence Hall of Science, University of California.

Chapter 4

Thoughts on Power and Pedagogy

Pat Rogers

> The fact that [the students] find me intimidating has been with me since day one of my teaching. The only explanation that I have about the disparity of this perception and 'the reality (= I am quite accessible)' is that I do not wish to be the student's 'pal' when I teach. On the one hand I wish to create the environment in which the students ask any questions and think any thoughts, unfettered, so they can learn. On the other hand they must be trained to think precisely and 'speak the truth'—they must learn that some of the things that they will think or say will be labeled as nonsense by someone. They cannot forever remain 'children'—some things will not be forgiven (after a certain time). Well you see the dilemma. I am just a 'stern and loving father' to them—a model of a father that is probably totally lost to the current American generation.
>
> (Private communication)

The teacher writing above is trying to come to terms with and account for the paradoxical situation in which he finds himself. Students flock to his courses, taking courses with him year after year, and yet describe him as intimidating, as 'striking fear in the hearts of undergraduates'. The reason they all give for continuing to take his courses is that they learn so much from him. As one female student explained to me: 'Sure you hate him while you're going through it, but, in retrospect you look back and "Wow! What a great teacher. I learned so much. I want to get him again!" ' And so when the class schedule comes out for the next semester, many students will 'look to see what he's teaching, then take it!'

This chapter explores the way power typically is used and how it can be used in the mathematics classroom to help students find their own voices and become independent mathematical thinkers. This discussion is based on my study of a particular mathematics programme in which I am seeking to understand the reasons for their success in influencing large numbers of students, a majority of them female, to choose a mathematical career and in supporting and retaining them in their studies.

BACKGROUND TO THE STUDY

Currently less than one per cent of all bachelor degrees granted in North America are in mathematics; at The State University of New York (SUNY) College at Potsdam the corresponding figure has been at least 20 per cent in each of the last four years. According to a Mathematical Association of America (MAA) survey (Albers *et al.*, 1987) for the period 1980–1985, while overall undergraduate enrolments in the United States remained relatively stable, there was an increase in the number of undergraduate mathematics degrees of 45 per cent; the corresponding figure for Potsdam was 152 per cent.

The success of the Potsdam Mathematics Department was first documented by the Committee on the Undergraduate Program in Mathematics (CUPM) of the MAA in a report where they were described as an example of a department which is successful in 'attracting a large number of students into a program that develops rigorous mathematical thinking and also offers a spectrum of (well taught) [sic] courses in pure and applied mathematics' (CUPM, 1981).

A small undergraduate institution serving about 4000 students, Potsdam College is situated close to the Canadian border in the north east corner of New York State, a rural area known as the North Country. From its early beginnings in 1816 the college had been involved primarily in teacher education until it became the State University College of Arts and Science at Potsdam in 1962.

According to admissions personnel, the college draws from a wide area of New York State, attracting students primarily from lower middle class backgrounds, often from farming communities and small villages. Students are invariably the first in their family to attend college. With no tradition of post-secondary education to support them, poor self-concept and low self-esteem is often a problem. The college population is 54 per cent female and admissions statistics for 1988 indicate that female and male students specifying mathematics as their major apply and are admitted in roughly equal numbers.

In 1983, 60.4 per cent of all Potsdam's mathematics degrees were awarded to women compared with 43.8 per cent nationally. (Degrees awarded to women in that year at Potsdam comprised 55 per cent of the total number of degrees awarded compared with 51 per cent nationally.) Furthermore, in five of the last seven years the top graduating student in the college as a whole has been a female mathematics major.

Ehrhart and Sandler, in a recent report of the Project on the Status and Education of Women (1987), conclude that the retention of women in traditionally male programmes at the post-secondary level is strongly linked with the quality of their college experiences. While women may have made considerable gains in equal access to post-secondary education, female students still have significantly fewer opportunities than their male peers to develop academic self-confidence and to have their academic goals and career aspirations validated by faculty and administrators.

> Behaviors and attitudes that express different expectations for women or single them out or ignore them because of their sex . . . can have a profound negative impact on women's academic and career development.
>
> (Ehrhart and Sandler, 1987, p. 5)

In 'A modern fairy tale?', Poland (1987, p. 294) discusses his impressions of the Potsdam College mathematics programme. He attributes its success to the way they are able to 'instill self-confidence and a sense of achievement'. Students he talked to said they felt the faculty cared for each one of them. Poland observed that the caring the students experienced resulted in their expressing a high degree of confidence in their own mathematical abilities. He speculated that this could be why 'they graduate more women in mathematics than men, that they address and redress a lack of confidence many women may feel about their ability to be mathematicians or to do mathematics competently' (Poland, 1987, p. 293).

DESCRIPTION OF THE STUDY

My investigation into the reasons for Potsdam's success with female students uses qualitative techniques to gather and analyse a variety of data. (For a discussion of the type of research techniques used in my study see, for example, Glaser and Strauss, 1967.) During my research, data collection and informal data analysis went hand in hand, with the emerging themes guiding further data collection. My interim findings were reported in two separate sessions to faculty and students and have been validated by both groups.

I began the study in April 1987 by interviewing a total of 32 female students and 8 male students. The interviews were relatively open-ended but were focused around my research question. Although I opened the interviews with some general questions, I made every effort not to lead the subjects but to allow them to shape the content of the interview. All but four interviews were conducted with pairs of students and most were of one hour's duration; one interview with two male students extended for an extra half-hour and, at my request, two female students agreed to a second individual interview (these students I regard as key informants and my purpose in talking to them again was to validate my emerging theory). The setting chosen for interviews was comfortable and quiet and communication and interaction among the interview pair was encouraged. Individual interviews were avoided because of the danger that interviewees might supply the answers they think the interviewer desires rather than the answers they wish to give.

In selecting interviewees I was greatly assisted by the present Chair of the department who at all times assumed a helpful but disinterested role in facilitating my research; 13 interviewees were selected by me and the remaining 27 were chosen by the Chair in accordance with my guidelines: initially I concentrated on female students with grade point averages (g.p.a.) of 3.25 or above on a 4-point scale, but later I expanded my sample to include male students as well as students with g.p.a.s below 3.25. A large proportion (13 out of 40) of the students I interviewed were also education majors who by virtue of their career aspirations are generally more sensitive to and aware of the teaching styles and teaching strategies of their teachers.

My interviews with the students were taped and I kept detailed notes of interviews with counselling, admissions and administrative personnel, and all mathematics department faculty members. As well, I observed office consultations between faculty and students and classroom situations.

In a study of this kind it is difficult not to bring certain expectations to the field—the essential task for the researcher is to avoid having these biases inform the findings. Poland rejected the view that 'teaching techniques' might explain Potsdam's success (Poland, 1987, p. 295), but I remained unconvinced. Indeed, my view now is that it is Potsdam's approach to teaching that is at the heart of their success, especially with their female students. I will elaborate on this later, but first I will discuss one factor about Potsdam that I did not expect to find.

HEROES, IDOLS AND PATRIARCHY

Given the importance placed by some writers on providing female students in male-dominated fields such as the mathematical sciences with female role models (Ehrhart and Sandler, 1987, p. 6), it surprised me to find that in a department of 15 staff, only one is female (this despite repeated recruitment efforts). I anticipated finding a department which was aware of the issue of underrepresentation of women in mathematics and which had taken deliberate steps to recruit female students and to meet their perceived special needs. Instead, I found an apparent patriarchy; a department of men—albeit men who are genuinely concerned about all students regardless of their gender—who exercise their authority as men in the classroom. Returning from a student function together, the teacher quoted at the start of the chapter once remarked to me: 'You've got the idea haven't you, I hope, that our students are more to us than just mathematical minds? . . . In this department, the men are men and the women are women and we're really up front about that. We're really interested in people as people—we're not just interested in the mind. Gender is part of the person, and it's not that we're going to be biased because someone is a woman or someone is a man. But it is absurd to say it's unimportant because gender is part of the person.'

Furthermore, the female students themselves expressed profound ignorance of the fact that females are often discouraged from taking mathematics. Only a few students admitted to being aware of the stereotyping of mathematics as a male domain. And certainly when they look around at Potsdam it is very female to study mathematics; for many of them this had also been their experience in high school.

A recurring theme in the interviews with female students is the 'teacher as father-figure'. I asked one student why she liked the teacher quoted at the start of this chapter when her description of him made him sound so intimidating. She laughed and replied, 'Yah, he's friendly about his intimidation . . . That's why [he] comes off more like a father . . . kind of nurturing you . . . like "Yes, you've made a mistake, but you haven't done anything that any of my other students haven't done." So I don't feel bad.' Other terms which are frequently used interchangeably with 'father-figure' are 'hero', 'idol', 'role-model', and 'mentor'. The faculty too refer to themselves as 'father-figures', as is typified by the opening quotation. However, as stern and demanding and challenging as these fathers can be, they can also be 'loving'. And it is this, I believe, this mixture of challenge and love, and the balance they are able to maintain between the two, that mitigates the negative consequences for females of studying within a patriarchal environment (Ehrhart and Sandler, 1987, pp. 5–7).

MATHEMATICS PEDAGOGY AND SUBJECTIVITY

The power of teachers generally resides in the fact that they control the transmission of skills and knowledge in terms of both form and content. They also control the means and methods of evaluation. In the case of mathematics teaching this power is further enhanced by students' mistaken beliefs and myths about mathematics. Most important among these is the notion that teachers possess a great deal of knowledge which can only be obtained from them and which they will impart only if the student obeys the rules.

There are many social and psychological pressures that contribute to mathematics avoidance by women. Recently, without denying or undervaluing the importance of these factors, a number of writers (see, for example, Buerk, 1985; Rogers, 1985; Burton, 1987) have come to recognize that a decisive factor is the way that mathematics has traditionally been presented and experienced in the classroom. Students at the secondary and post-secondary levels are rarely given the opportunity to play with ideas in mathematics and to construct their own meanings and understanding. They are presented with mathematics through textbooks and the polished lectures, where mathematics is made to appear a finished, absolute and predigested product. A pedagogy that emphasizes product deprives students of experiencing the process by which ideas in mathematics come to be and perpetuates a dualistic view of mathematics in which right answers are known by authorities and are the property of experts (Perry, 1970, 1981). Such a pedagogy strips mathematics of the context in which it was created and is based on misconceptions about its very nature.

Gilligan's (1982) research in the field of women's moral development provides a link between mathematics avoidance and mathematics pedagogy. She identified two styles of reasoning which, although not gender-specific, are thought by some to be gender-related: one, the traditional style, is characterized by objectivity, reason, logic, and appeal to justice; and the other, 'the different voice', often identified with women and consequently devalued, is characterized by subjectivity, intuition, and a desire to maintain relationships.

Buerk (1985) has identified these styles in the work of mathematicians. At a colloquium of the Mathematics Department of Ithaca College she presented participants with a list of 'excerpts from Gilligan's book, juxtaposing phrases characterizing "separate" reasoning with some which characterized "connected" reasoning' (Buerk, 1985, p. 63). The consensus was that the 'connected' list represented the way mathematicians do mathematics. 'Mathematics is intuitive,' they said. They stressed . . . [that doing mathematics is a creative process requiring] 'attention to the limitations and exceptions to theories, the connections between ideas, and the search for differences among theories and patterns that appear similar. And yet they agreed that the "separate" list conveyed the way that mathematics is communicated in the classroom, in textbooks, and in their professional writing' (Buerk, 1985, p. 64).

The point is that mathematicians employ both forms of reasoning in their creative work. But the problem with the way mathematics is so often taught, particularly at the tertiary level where the lecture mode of instruction is so predominant, is that students are not given the opportunity to be involved in the journey: the process of constructing mathematical ideas where 'connected' thought is so important. Thus there is an enormous cognitive gulf between the style in which mathematics is presented and the way in which students are best able to construct their own understanding of it. Some students are able to bridge this gap for themselves but many are not. Bridging this gap requires initiative, independence of thought and risk-taking, the very skills possessed by effective problem-solvers, and the very skills that are discouraged in the young female.

Another reason why the expository mode of presentation may adversely affect women more than men is because it uses and appeals to authority as a means of imparting knowledge. Power in the lecture situation resides with the speaker and few students are able to cultivate their own voice. However, there are marked gender differences in relationship with authorities (Belenky *et al.*, 1986, pp. 43–5). Males are encouraged from an early age to challenge authority and receive support for holding the floor and presenting their own views. Women, on the other hand, are encouraged to subordinate their own voice to that of authorities and are far less likely than men to maintain a sense of their own autonomy. Ehrhart and Sandler (1987, p. 6) argue that not only are the physical sciences often 'dominated by men in terms of numbers, but their operating procedures, values, and power structures could be termed "masculine" in the sense that they emphasize hierarchy, individual prowess, and highly assertive behavior instead of cooperation'. Thus the mathematical experience of most female undergraduates is dominated by males employing authoritarian modes of communication to which they often respond in customary silence.

PORTRAIT OF AN EMPOWERING TEACHER

The teacher quoted at the start of the chapter does not believe that only the gifted and talented few are capable of becoming mathematicians. Instead he tells his students that they are all capable of learning mathematics, provided they are prepared to work hard. He sees his job as identifying 'the needs and level of understanding of his students and [finding] a way to help them learn what they need to know'. For what purpose? He says, 'So that they might learn to think precisely and speak the truth'. Note that he did not say '*learn* the truth' but '*speak* the truth'. The focus here is on developing your own voice through which to express what you know in a way that is true, rather than developing skills at passively absorbing material thought to be important for you to learn.

How does this teacher teach his students to speak the truth? Not by subscribing to the 'banking' concept of education in which the teacher's role 'is to "fill" the students by making deposits of information which the teachers consider to consitute true knowledge' (Freire, 1971, p. 63). Instead his goal 'is to make [the students] independent of [him] and any other teacher'. In his opening remarks at the start of a new course he warns his students that 'we should tell you as little as possible and help you to read your text[book]'. He sees his role as 'providing opportunities for the students to think up and write down correct proofs and appropriate counterexamples . . . to do little for you, and give opportunities [for you] to do a lot for yourself'.

In this teacher's class there is almost no lecturing. Most of the time, students are working together informally in small groups, discussing problems, arguing, negotiating meaning. The teacher walks around, looking over shoulders, asking questions. From time to time he sends a student to the board to write up her solution. Then there is some discussion with the student-teacher taking a leading role. The class may end with a brief lecture on some new material or an assignment of new problems to be taken up at the next meeting.

This teacher shares the journey of recreating mathematics with his students. He believes that students need to know they are capable of intelligent thought, not as a reward for finishing the course successfully, but as a prerequisite for engaging in it productively. The role of expert in his classes shifts between teacher and student. The stage is shared and as the drama unfolds the students learn that theories are not the sole property of experts, rather they develop the ability to reconstruct them for themselves. In this way, the teacher supports the growth and evolution of the students' thinking and helps them discover their own voices. In his class, knowledge is not the private and exclusive property of the teacher, but is negotiated in a community of trust where confidence and self-esteem are protected.

Power in mathematics resides with those who have knowledge of process. With such knowledge the student becomes independent of the teacher, not needing him for approval, or for confirmation. The Potsdam faculty actively encourage this independence in their students in a variety of ways: by true acceptance of the students they have rather than the students they might wish they had (I heard no complaints of the 'If only we had better students!' variety); by having their students model as 'expert' and trusting them to learn from the experience; by teaching the students how to read a mathematics book; by encouraging collaborative learning and peer tutoring; and by respecting the students' ultimate right to personal responsibility for their own learning.

TEACHING AS COACHING

The teacher's role at Potsdam is that of coach. In my classroom observations I did not observe a singular 'Potsdam teaching technique'; indeed, the advising materials for students explicitly refer to the existence of a variety of teaching styles and they see this multiplicity as one of the programme's strengths. However, a common theme of the many metaphors that are used by the faculty and by the students to describe what goes on in the classroom is that the Potsdam teacher is a coach and the student is a mathematician-in-training. These metaphors signal a very different philosophy of mathematics teaching from the traditional one which emphasizes exposing the student to the professor's perspective on a specific body of material.

In the traditional lecture mode of teaching mathematics at the undergraduate level, the student has no control over what she learns or how she learns it. (In keeping with the reality of Potsdam and the theme, I shall continue to refer to teachers as male and students as female.) The focus is on the transmission of knowledge rather than the development of skills in the student. As well, since there is often a large amount of material that is considered to be important in a course, thoughtful reflection and application of the ideas and concepts is often postponed indefinitely in the interests of 'mastering' the essential information. Students have insufficient time to assimilate new concepts before their properties and consequences are deduced.

Potsdam professors believe that material conveyed in this way invariably is quickly forgotten when the course is over. Their teaching practices show that students who learn to think mathematically are able to reconstruct ideas and learn independently and that this skill, like riding a bicycle, is never forgotten. But teaching in this way demands a commitment from the teacher to give the students time outside of class and it also demands that the teacher make careful decisions about what is essential in the curriculum. Not everything can be 'covered' in class. Although the students may be made responsible for the entire curriculum in a course, the professor will select and treat those topics he considers to be essential or best suited to develop the students' ability to think mathematically.

This attitude towards teaching requires a 'caring teacher'. I use the term 'caring' not simply as a feeling of concern, attentiveness or solicitude for another person, but in the very specific sense of 'caring' as in helping 'the other grow and actualize [her]self' (Mayeroff, 1971). The Potsdam teacher: 'receive[s] the student, [and] looks at the subject matter with [her]. [His] commitment is to [her], the cared-for, and [s]he is—through that commitment—set free to pursue [her] legitimate projects' (Noddings, 1984, p. 177).

In caring for the growth and development of a student, a teacher must experience the student as having worth in her own right and the potential and the need to grow. (These remarks are based in part on Mayeroff's book *On Caring* and summarize those aspects of caring that are descriptive of the teachers I have observed at Potsdam.) As well, the teacher must recognize that the student needs him in order to grow. However, he must desire neither to dominate nor to manipulate the student—he will not always impose his own direction, but will also follow the lead of the student. To do this effectively, the teacher must know the student's level of development in order that he can devise ways to help her grow. The caring teacher trusts the student to grow in her own time and in her own way, and he is patient because he believes in and trusts in the student's ability to grow, to make mistakes and to learn from them. He will actively promote and safeguard conditions that are favourable to his students' growth.

CONCLUSION

The teacher I have described here has made no particular effort to attract female students and no specific adaptations to meet their perceived special needs. In this, his is typical of the approach of all mathematics teachers at Potsdam College. Indeed, gender does not appear to be at all a factor in their teaching, neither directly or indirectly. No research has yet proved that there are inherent reasons why women should not be successful mathematicians. On the contrary, the evidence provided by the Potsdam mathematics programme suggests that, in an environment that is genuinely open to and supportive of *all* students and in which the style of teaching is true to the nature of mathematical inquiry, women are attracted to mathematics and are just as successful as men.

However, for me, and for my readers who are interested in feminist pedagogy, my findings are discomforting and indicate that we may need to think more deeply about power and authority. How is it that a group of 'stern but loving fathers', caring but traditional fathers none the less, can succeed so well in empowering women? Perhaps it is because their motive in wielding their authority is that they might later relinquish it—and in this they truly differ from the typical patriarch and his aims.

ACKNOWLEDGEMENT

I wish to acknowledge and thank the Social Sciences and Humanities Research Council of Canada for financial support and my friend Leslie Sanders for helping me to clarify my ideas in this paper.

REFERENCES

Albers, D.J., Anderson, R.D. and Loftsgaarden, D.O. (1987) *Undergraduate Programs in the Mathematical and Computer Sciences: the 1985-86 Survey*. MAA Notes, Number 7.

Belenky, M.F., B.M. Clinchy, N.R. Goldberger and J.M. Tarule (1986) *Women's Ways of Knowing: The Development of Self, Voice and Mind*. New York: Basic Books.

Buerk, D. (1985) The voices of women making meaning in mathematics. *Journal of Education*, **167**(3), 59-70.

Burton, L. (1987) Women and mathematics: Is there an intersection? *IOWME Newsletter*, **3**(1), 4-7.

CUPM Report (1981) *Recommendations for a General Mathematical Sciences Program*. Mathematical Association of America.

Ehrhart, J.K. and Sandler, B.R. (1987) *Looking for More Than a Few Good Women in Traditionally Male Fields*. Project on the Status and Education of Women. Washington, DC: Association of American Colleges.

Freire, P. (1971) *Pedagogy of the Oppressed*. New York: Seaview.

Gilligan, C. (1982) *In a Different Voice: Psychological Theory and Women's Development*. Cambridge, MA: Harvard University Press.

Glaser, B.G. and Strauss, A.L. (1967) *The Discovery of Grounded Theory: Strategies for Qualitative Research*. New York: Aldine.

Mayeroff, M. (1971) *On Caring*. New York: Harper & Row.

Noddings, N. (1984) *Caring*. Berkeley, CA: University of California Press.

Perry, W.G., Jr (1970) *Forms of Intellectual and Ethical Development in the College Years: A Scheme*. New York: Holt, Rinehart & Winston.

Perry, W.G., Jr (1981) Cognitive and ethical growth: The making of meaning, in Chickering, A. (ed.) *The Modern American College*. San Francisco: Josey-Bass, pp. 76-116.

Poland, J. (1987) A modern fairy tale? *American Mathematical Monthly*, **94**(3), 291-5.

Rogers, P. (1985) Overcoming another barrier: real women don't do math—with good reason! *Canadian Woman Studies Journal*, **6**(4), 82-4.

Chapter 5

American Female and Male University Professors' Mathematical Attitudes and Life Histories

Lyn Taylor

This study sought to discover what effect different educational, interpersonal and intellectual experiences had on twelve professors' attitudes toward mathematics and their career choice. Were there meaningful differences between the female and male professors' experiences? Part of the purpose was to utilize a qualitative methodology that is not often used in exploring such issues in the hope that it would yield new information.

The participants included eight mathematics professors and four social scientists. All received their doctorates between 1976 and 1986 and have reputations as excellent classroom teachers at universities in the southwestern United States. Six were females and six were males. Table 5.1 further introduces the participants by their pseudonyms, detailing their birth year, ethnicity, gender, and degrees.

In-depth interviews with the participants during 1986–1987 involved both open-ended and focused questions concerning their mathematical life histories and attitudes. An important value of this qualitative research is the use of the participants' words to provide an inside view of their reality. One strength of this research is the detailed descriptions of the participants' experiences, thoughts, and feelings. A limitation is that the findings are relevant for these participants and should not to be generalized to other populations. However, they may be used to generate theories to be tested in future studies.

This chapter focuses on the findings related to gender. These major areas include: parental and teacher influence, peers in the classroom, the career, confidence, and attributions. Some of the themes explored involve parental attitudes, teachers, classroom experiences, discrimination, advising, sex role socialization, ability, doubts, and effort.

PARENTAL AND TEACHER INFLUENCE

The detailed accounts of the participants' families and relationships with teachers showed the depth of influence of these persons in the participants' development and perception of themselves as learners of mathematics. Fennema (1981) has found

Table 5.1. *Participants' demographic information.*

Name	Birth year, Ethnicity*, gender†	Bachelor's degree	Master's degree	Terminal degree
Becca	1938 A F	Univ. Kansas BA Mathematics	Univ. Kansas MA Mathematics	American Univ. PhD Mathematics Educ.
Carolyn	1929 A F	Purdue Univ. BS Mathematics	Univ. Nebraska-Omaha MS Mathematics	Univ. Nebraska-Lincoln PhD Mathematics Educ.
Kathy	1950 A F	Gettysburg College BA English Lit.	Univ. New Mexico MA Mathematics	Univ. New Mexico PhD Mathematics
Fabi	1948 C F	Eastern New Mexico BA Mathematics	Univ. Washington MEd Mathematics Educ.	Harvard Univ. EdD Mathematics Educ.
Bjorn	1949 A M	Univ. Colorado BA Mathematics	Harvard Univ. MS Applied Math	Harvard Univ. PhD Applied Math
Cleofus	1950 B M	Bucknell College BS Elect. Engin.	Johns Hopkins Univ. MS Numerical Analysis New Mexico Tech. MS Mathematics	Univ. New Mexico PhD Mathematics
Reuben	1956 A M	Mass. Inst. Tech. BS Mathematics	Univ. Calif. L. A. MA Mathematics	Univ. Calif. L. A. PhD Mathematics
Ed	1950 A M	Boston College BS Mathematics	Boston College MA Mathematics	Oregon St. Univ. PhD Mathematics
Fred	1944 N M	Fort Lewis College BS Humanities Education	Univ. New Mexico MA Elem. Educ. Bilingual Educ.	Univ. New Mexico EdD Elem. Educ. Multi-Disciplinary
Gerry	1951 A M	Indiana Univ. BA History	Indiana Univ. MA Sociology	Indiana Univ. PhD Sociology
Sylvia	1950 A F	Colorado St. Univ. BA Sociology Philosophy	Colorado St. Univ. MA Sociology Philosophy	Brown Univ. PhD Sociology
Vera	1950 A F	Lewis & Clark College BA History	Western Oregon St. MA Extreme Learning Problems	U.S. International Univ. EdD Curric. & Inst.

* Ethnicity codes: A, Anglo; B, Black; C, Chicana; N, Native American.
† Gender codes: F, female; M, male.

parental and teacher attitudes toward the student as a learner of mathematics are influential. In this study they were also found to be influential.

Education was highly valued in all the families. The parents encouraged and supported their sons' and daughters' education, yet they did not push them toward any particular academic discipline. They exposed the participants to many things, provided an environment where education was readily available and valued, and let their children develop and pursue their own interests. With the exception of one father who seemed threatened by his academically gifted daughter (as well as by his son, other daughter, and wife), the participants perceived their parents to be very supportive of their learning and education.

The participants' development was positively encouraged by supportive and caring relationships with knowledgeable teachers. Some of these teachers opened up the beautiful world of mathematics for their students, piquing their curiosity, encouraging them, and exciting their interest to pursue learning mathematics.

And conversely, some of their teachers' negative and boring portrayals of mathematics presented a rather uninteresting subject for the participants to pursue. A prime example of this was Cleofus's junior high mathematics teacher who dragged herself to class the last period of the day and 'blopped down' looking like she was in 'such pain' and said 'where were we'. Cleofus remarked 'you can imagine how we felt'. This unenthusiastic presentation of mathematics certainly did not inspire Cleofus.

'Teachers are the most important educational influence on students' learning of mathematics' (Fennema and Sherman, 1978). They influence students in many ways; a very significant one is sex role socialization. Fennema and Sherman (1978) believe that:

> Part of the teachers' influence is on the learners' development of sex role standards. These sex role standards include definitions of acceptable achievement in the various subject areas. It is believed that this influence by teachers is exerted through differential treatment of the sexes as well as expectations of sex-related differences in achievement.
>
> (pp. 13–14)

In this study the most pronounced example of sexism was exhibited by Sylvia's freshman calculus instructor. I feel it is essential to digress to tell Sylvia's story because it had such a profound effect on her development. Sylvia's frustrations with her calculus course helped cause her to pursue a major in sociology rather than mathematics. At 'that point I was still thinking about mathematics as a major'. Her frustrations were not caused by the subject as much as they were by the teacher. 'I got into a class of 60 people. [There were] two women and the man told us the first day that women shouldn't be in math and he was going to do everything to flunk us. The first exam I did everything right but I made a mistake, I multiplied 2×2 and got 2 on the problem, and he gave me a C on it. On the second midterm I also made a careless mistake, just a computational error, but I did the proofs right and he gave me a C – . I got so mad that I wouldn't go to class anymore. I was too dumb to drop the class. I didn't know, I was just a first semester freshman, I didn't know how it worked. I was too mad to go. I talked to him two or three times.'

Sylvia felt he was very sexist and unfair to her. 'He would say "You shouldn't be in this class, you are a woman, you shouldn't be in math, I don't know how you slipped by this far, but you shouldn't be here"'. He didn't tell me to drop it he just told me that he was going to flunk me. I know his name too, I'll never forget him. On the day of the final, having not been in class for the last third of the semester, I decided to take it anyway. Somehow I managed to pass the final. I ended up with a D in the class.' Fortunately, for future students, this teacher's contract was not renewed.

This experience had a dramatic effect on Sylvia and her career. 'It was the only D I ever got in college; actually, it was the only grade in college I got that wasn't an A. That experience itself made me decide not to go into mathematics.' Sylvia never took another mathematics class and after that 'I always resented math'. She did pursue statistics and social science research courses. 'I transferred my quantitative bent into philosophy and statistics.' Sylvia's doctoral programme was in quantitative sociology. She now uses statistics and the computer as tools for doing her research. Her research interests have also expanded into more theoretical areas and she now uses qualitative methodology as well as quantitative.

Carolyn also felt she did not receive much support in her first doctoral program because she was a woman and an older returning student. While Carolyn was doing well in her graduate mathematics courses, she felt discriminated against, 'too old' to be a doctoral student in mathematics, and very alone. 'I remember how hard it was to go back . . . I had not studied mathematics for fifteen years . . . almost too old to go back and get a doctorate.' She believes that she was discouraged from pursuing a doctorate in mathematics because she was an older female student. When she switched over to mathematics education doctoral program she was treated very differently: 'I was getting some encouragement too which I was not getting in the math department.' While these were the only two blatant examples of gender discrimination mentioned by the participants, it is likely there were many more subtle messages that were internalized without the participants being aware of them.

Hopefully there is less discrimination today. Certainly there are more women in careers involving mathematics than ever before. Becca thinks mathematics is 'an excellent field for women' and 'there are lots of avenues opening up, more than there used to be . . . Computers, . . . business . . . Teaching used to be the main avenue that was open, but I don't think that is true any more. I think that maybe the age discrimination is worse than the gender discrimination in mathematics.' None of the male participants reported having experienced discrimination. It would be interesting to know if older returning male students felt discriminated against.

PEERS IN THE CLASSROOM

During the course of the interviews Cleofus, Bjorn, Ed, Fred, Reuben, and Gerry all spoke about the number of bright female students that were in their mathematics classes through the years. For example, Cleofus said 'I thought the girls did better in math and got more attention than the guys. But I think that is because we were always playing around . . . In my experience they were always the serious ones. I thought they would be the real scholars and students.'

Cleofus went to an all boys high school so he couldn't comment on females in mathematics at that level. However, he said 'in junior high the girls were the best. If I had a question and the teacher was not around I would ask one of the girls. Back in those days they were the serious ones and the teachers did pay attention to them. But now it seems it is the opposite. You hear a lot about people not encouraging women in math and science. I think it is a strange situation. Given my experience I find it hard to believe that people don't believe that women are good in math and science. Hard to swallow. Women are not pointed in the direction of math when they are young. Math just doesn't seem to be an option. Also if you get a couple of bad teachers, no matter who you are, you aren't going to like math very much. If your parents didn't like it then that is going to add to it.' Cleofus's statement emphasized the important roles teachers and parents play in affecting students' attitudes toward mathematics and particularly in not encouraging female students to pursue mathematics. He points out the absence of positive expectations for the female students.

When Bjorn was asked about the treatment of students in mathematics courses he felt his peers were treated as individuals. 'No, I don't really have any recollection of differential treatment. In fact, I do have recollections of several girls, particularly in grade school, who were very good in math and that went on even through high school. I can remember girls in those classes who were far better in math than I was. Now I happen to know that some of those girls aren't doing anything remotely related to math now. Why? Perhaps they were not encouraged, perhaps they were in fact discouraged from going into a field like that. I can't say that for sure but I know they were very talented in math in all of my junior and high school math classes.'

Fred was also aware that the girls in his high school were very bright but observed 'the girls got sorted out to the point where there were none'. His high school trigonometry class was only males while his geometry class had two females and about ten males. His trigonometry class was 'by invitation' of the teacher and Fred believes 'I don't think he approached any girls'. Fred graduated from high school in the early 1960s.

Ed felt the bright female students he knew were not discouraged, yet he was aware that very few of them continued with their study of mathematics. 'We had some fairly bright females who were good in math and were never discouraged from being good in math, but I don't think they really went on to college in math. There weren't many who continued but they were not put down. Some of the best mathematical students in graduate school with the sharpest minds were females.' In reading these comments I wondered if, perhaps, when there was not discouragement there was a lack of encouragement and lessened expectations for the female students.

It was intriguing that all the men spoke about the bright female mathematics students they had known and none of the women in the study spoke about this. Of course, it is important to be aware the question was never directly asked of any of the participants. It is possible the male participants raised this issue because of my gender as a woman. The men's comments about the smart female students came up at three different times. One was while they were discussing their educational histories. The other two times were when the questions were related to gender. The question, 'If you were advising a woman who wanted to pursue mathematics, what would you tell her?' and the question 'How were the students treated in your math classes?' were asked of each of the participants after they had been discussing their opinions of the mathematics curriculum. These questions were carefully asked in this general way so the participants would comment on any differential treatment they had observed. This could include any differences. It was thought gender and ethnic differences might likely be mentioned. No ethnic differences were mentioned in regard to the treatment of students. Three of the participants in this study are of minority ethnicity yet none of them reported they had been discriminated against. It is possible this is related to the researcher's ethnicity as an Anglo.

Several participants (both male and female) spoke of the boys getting in trouble more often, but only the males spoke of how bright some of the females were. When I became aware of this while analysing the transcripts, I was surprised. Reflecting upon this observation I wonder if the women in the study just assumed there are many women who are bright mathematically and did not feel they needed to say it. Closely related to this, Fabi spoke of her concern that poor teaching caused many intelligent students 'to go down the drain' mathematically. It was implied but not stated that these students were both male and female.

The educational histories reveal all the participants had diverse academic interests. None of them was strictly focused on their academic area (mathematics or social science) to the exclusion of other subjects. All twelve professors pursued coursework in liberal arts.

The mathematics professors' interest in mathematics did not develop at the same time in their lives; they expressed an interest during their elementary and secondary educations. Three of the women became seriously interested in mathematics in high school and went to college as mathematics majors. However, only two of these women graduated with their bachelors' degrees in mathematics. Kathy earned her bachelors' degree in English. By contrast, three of the four men started their college education as engineering majors.

GENDER AND THE CAREER

While women have been underrepresented in mathematics for many years the times are changing. In a recent interview, Nobel Laureate Isidor I. Rabi (1987) spoke of how many more women were in science and mathematics today and said 'I wonder how much longer it will be that we will refer to a female scientist rather than just saying a scientist'. His comment deeply touched me. I was pleased that a man of his generation was so aware and concerned with equity issues. When you put this comment in a historical perspective, women have come a long way since Rabi was born in the late nineteenth century.

Gerry felt strongly that this is an excellent time for a woman to be pursuing math. 'The demographics are perfect for it right now. If she is a person that has an interest and some talents in those directions, it makes more sense than it has ever before. We now have laws in place and I think there have been changes in terms of acceptance of women in math and engineering in the last fifteen years. It is a sellers' market right now; so I think it is a great idea. You always want to be in a situation where you are a commodity that is in demand and I think it makes perfect sense. I certainly would encourage it.'

When Gerry was asked what advice he would give to a man wanting to pursue mathematics his response highlighted the gender differences and the difficulty of balancing a career and family. 'I think it is easier for a man because you don't have to buck the tradition; I think men are more likely to grow up thinking they would go into math than women are. Certainly that has been the case in the past. I think too, there is probably a price to pay for women in professions, in general. When I think about it I just don't know that many academic women who are married and have families; I think it is very difficult to do both, especially and be at the really top notch universities; that is not limited to math. There may be some truth to that saying that you have to be twice as good to compete if you are either a minority or a women. . . . Changing for women but not fast.' Gerry and his wife (a math teacher) try to balance their careers and family, sharing equally in the child and household responsibilities.

The response given by Gerry showed there are many complex factors that affect a person's sex-role socialization and development. Certainly, there are no simple answers. The responses of all twelve participants indicated they would strongly encourage any student who was interested in mathematics to pursue it regardless of their gender or race. The key element they all emphasized was that the person be interested and motivated in mathematics.

In advising a woman who wanted to pursue mathematics, Bjorn would tell her 'If you like it, pursue it'. He'd tell a man the same thing. 'I have just never understood the division that takes place between the sexes. I guess I can believe that at one time it was encouraged—maybe in grade schools, junior highs. (It is not) something that I have sensed at all as a teacher. I look at a woman or a man in my class and mathematically they are identical. I've seen many mathematicians who are women. Now, the fact that they are outnumbered is a historical fact. I think the numbers are becoming more and more equal. There is no reason to doubt the mathematical abilities of women!'

When Cleofus was asked about advising a woman who was interested in pursuing mathematics he responded first with a surprised look and a question 'As opposed to a man?' He feels 'maybe I am kind of blind to the sexism part, but I just don't see that due to my background'. He then spoke of the advice he would give her or him: 'For someone who is generally interested in math—do your homework in respect to what kind of college, and make sure you find a good advisor. . . . Think of math as not so much competition. Think if you apply yourself there should not be a problem.' It was interesting that Cleofus's response indicated the importance of finding a good advisor and having a positive confident attitude. He was the only one focusing on those areas in answering this particular question. All the rest of the participants mentioned they would give a student, woman or man, the same advice and that the most important thing is to pursue what one finds interesting.

CONFIDENCE

The National Council of Teachers of Mathematics (1989) has said one of the most important goals reflected in their mathematics curriculum standards is 'becoming confident in one's ability mathematically' (p. 12). Confidence has been reported by many researchers (Helson, 1967; Fennema, 1981, 1987; Becker, 1984; Reyes, 1984; Steen, 1987; and others) to be one of the most important variables related to mathematical learning. Reyes (1984) said 'confidence in one's ability to learn mathematics appears consistently as a strong predictor of mathematics course election' (p. 562). Yet, research by Becker (1984) with graduate students in mathematics and Helson (1967) with creative mathematicians showed the females lacked confidence in their mathematical abilities. The males in these studies were markedly more confident in their mathematical abilities than the females.

Confidence appears to have a basis in experience. The participants' comments caused me to think about the possible relationships among confidence, ability, and experience. It is possible that successful experiences and ability may be strong predictors of confidence. These relationships are interesting areas for future research.

One major finding of this study involves the male and female college mathematics teachers' confidence. Their comments indicated that there were no marked differences in confidence between the female and male professors in this study. While all the participants expressed confidence in their mathematical abilities, they also spoke about levels of confidence and pointed out that mathematics is a 'humbling discipline'. While they all had confidence at a certain level, they all expressed the same doubts and concerns at other levels or in other areas of mathematics.

For example, Fabi said 'I think math is a humbling discipline. Just when you think you know everything you could possibly know somebody will come up with some little problem and you think that it should be simple and yet it will be mind boggling, so I don't know. . . . I think there will always be little twist to a problem that I haven't thought of and I'll be puzzled about it—which is nice; it really keeps you on your toes.' There seemed to be a certain amount of intrigue about that 'little twist'.

When asked how confident he felt about mathematics, Bjorn thoughtfully responded 'Well, that is a hard question. For one thing I think it is a mistake to feel overly confident about anything. . . . that is an attitude that I would try not to cultivate anyway. I am not sure I have ever strived for it. What is confidence in mathematics? You know you feel confident about mathematics at some level, (but) all you have to do is lift your sights a few degrees and you will find an area of mathematics that you have no confidence. So, confidence is a relative thing; to me it is almost meaningless.'

Another important aspect of confidence emerging strongly during the interviews was their confidence relative to teaching. For instance Bjorn said 'Now confidence, I think, is an important aspect of teaching. I think that any teacher can tell you the difference between a lecture that is given with a sense of confidence and a lecture that is given without that confidence. I think that is a significant factor to the extent that it improves one's teaching, I think confidence is probably an important factor, but to feel that you have confidence in the absolute sense is almost meaningless.'

For the participants, confidence in teaching was closely tied to their preparation for class. Fabi stressed 'You can't go to a math class unprepared'. Cleofus accentuated 'being prepared' was essential for good teaching. Reuben, Ed, Bjorn, Becca, Kathy, and Carolyn emphasized they spent many hours preparing for their classes. Quite often they would spend a lot of time during the summer preparing for a new class they were to teach in the fall. Carolyn's response typified their sense of confidence 'I don't think I have ever felt unconfident about anything I have taught'. With teaching a subject they developed greater confidence in their teaching and a more thorough understanding of it. All the participants stressed this. It is important to remember all these professors are known for being excellent teachers.

Confidence was also tied to their research and presentations about it. For Cleofus his dissertation defence was a peak professional experience that helped him to develop more confidence in both his ability to do and to present research 'When I gave my defense it worked very well—people liked it and I could answer all their questions and it made sense. I was a little nervous. I thought "this is it". But, I was told I was the expert in this and realized I was and that helped a lot.' Fabi also spoke about developing confidence in her research and felt completing her dissertation was like having a 'black cloud' lifted. Not unexpectedly, the positive experience of completing successful research projects increased the confidence of all the participants in their abilities to do research.

Again and again the transcripts revealed there were relative levels of confidence in teaching and research. Ed said 'On the graduate level of teaching I feel fairly confident. But, plunging off into the unknown and coming up with a "result" I am not terribly thrilled.' Part of this relative confidence seems inherent in the nature of mathematics. For mathematicians to have publishable results they have to have proved something new. As Ed pointed out, this is not the case in all fields, 'I have twinges of jealousy with people in chemistry who can set up an experiment and even if the experiment doesn't generate the results they vie for they can still write it up. But if you start out in an area of math and try to prove something you don't write up your failures. "Well I wanted to prove this but I didn't get anywhere," you just can't do that.'

Bjorn's response typified the relative levels of ability in mathematics the participants were aware of 'I think that anybody who does math can look around them and see people that seem to be, and probably are, a lot more adept at doing mathematics than they are. That is an ongoing process. Anybody in mathematics should be able to look around and find another mathematician that he admires. . . . The point is there is no upper bound to excellence in mathematics! Even the best of mathematicians can look somewhere, either historically or among their peers, and find someone that is deserving of respect.'

When asked if he had experienced any difficult times with mathematics that stood out in his mind, Bjorn was quick to say 'Sure, research does not come easy for me at all and I'm not sure what I mean by difficult. Not difficult in the sense of being demoralizing necessarily, but difficult in the sense of having to work hard. Then, I would say that much of the research I do is in that category.' Sometimes, Bjorn finds it difficult to prepare new graduate course lectures. 'It is difficulty in the sense of being a challenge, and to me that is inspiring and I think strong motivation, too.' It appears even confident mathematicians have difficult times and doubts. While this may seem obvious to some, it is not to many students.

Ed spoke of his higher confidence level for teaching and learning mathematics and lower confidence relative to research 'I don't have a very high opinion of myself as a math researcher but as a math learner and expositor. Somewhere along the line I wrote an essay on WHY—explaining how I loved math, etc. But, I don't think I will have a theorem named after me!'

The amount of confidence the participants expressed seemed directly tied to their level of effort in a specific area. They had consciously made decisions about where they would direct their efforts. For example, Ed said 'I don't think I am directed toward research-based things. . . . What I do is directed toward teaching methods or involving students in math.'

Confidence was important to the male and female professors in three areas: teaching, learning, and research. From the above descriptions it seems confidence is not a constant but related to the levels of effort and interest of the mathematicians. There did not seem to be any gender-related differences in the levels of confidence expressed. The females were as confident as the males in the areas to which they directed their energies. All the participants expressed concern over their doubts. This appears to be another indicator of their confidence. I believe that a confident person is more comfortable and likely to discuss their doubts. I am convinced, as are Gilligan (1982) and Fennema (1981), that females are often more open than males to expressing their feelings and doubts. American males are typically socialized to be 'strong' and not show any doubts or signs of 'weakness'. The fact that all the males in this study were able to express their doubts could be an indicator of their confidence. It also seems likely that this quality may be related to these twelve professors being excellent teachers.

ATTRIBUTIONS

After a thorough review of the literature Reyes (1984) reported there is 'a well-established relationship between attributions and achievement-related behaviors such as persistence, effort, and choice of challenging tasks' (p. 568). She says this work assumes those putting in more effort achieve at higher levels. Reyers reported gender differences in patterns of attribution of success and failure in that females are 'more likely to see success as caused by effort and less likely to see success as caused by ability' (p. 568).

Looking specifically at mathematics attribution studies using the Mathematics Attribution Scale (MAS) developed by Fennema, Wolleat, and Pedro revealed some similar findings. In a study of 647 female and 577 male high school students, Pedro *et al.* (1981) found males, more often than females, attributed their success in mathematics to ability, and females, more often than males, attributed their success to effort.

While this study is different from the one cited above, it is of interest to note all eight of the college mathematics teachers attributed their success in mathematics to effort. It is recognized the college mathematics teachers in this study are older than the high school students and it is therefore inappropriate to compare the two groups and say this is a major finding. It is therefore noted merely as a finding of interest and an area for future research.

The eight college mathematics teachers in this study were each asked 'To what do you attribute your success in mathematics?' Persistence and hard work were the answers most given by both the females and the males. Both persistence and hard work are components of effort.

When ability was mentioned at all, it was cited as secondary. For instance Cleofus responded 'Hard work! That is number one and two. Need some intelligence; I think that is part of it—mostly hard work for me.' Kathy replied 'Patience, endurance, persistence, a willingness to take care of detail, maybe ability. I don't know if it is a willingness or an ability.' When asked to explain this further she responded 'I'm not a genius. So, I make up for that lack of genius through persistence. . . . I probably have a touch of it. Some people can just seem to rely on it.'

These feelings of humble modesty and a lack of 'genius' have been reported by other mathematicians. For instance, Halmos (1985), a distinguished professor of mathematics who has written ten books and over 100 articles, said 'I am not a genius. I just enjoyed it and fooled around with it' (p. 122). He also spoke of how hard he worked.

In a similar fashion Reuben responded 'Perseverance! I don't think I have overwhelming talent. I have talent but not that sharp. I don't see clever things that quickly. When I think about something for a long time I can understand it very well. My own math doesn't have clever proofs but gets down to what is really going on underneath something. I believe that it has a certain amount of depth; I think it comes from staying on the subject, persevering when you run into difficulties and continuing to work on the situation. So, for me I'd say perseverence more than pure talent.' Newton, when asked how he made his discoveries is supposed to have answered, 'by thinking on them continually'. Focused effort was extended to create success.

It is likely a certain amount of ability was taken for granted by the other participants and they felt it was not something to mention. Humble modesty was displayed in all the responses. They were all proud of what they had accomplished so far but felt they still had more goals ahead of them. Both the female and male professors appeared to be high achieving persons who set high standards for themselves.

SUMMARY

I will summarize the important gender-related themes that emerged from their individual stories, themes that I believe are significant in the development of their positive attitudes toward mathematics and teaching, as well as their career choices. The formation of an attitude is a complex process that involves the interaction of a number of factors and cannot be explained simply or completely.

One might presume that there might be greater differences between the female and male professors of mathematics and social science in this study. I found more similarities than differences between them.

This particular group of twelve participants have first and foremost in common their love of teaching and a strong sense of identity that developed based, in part, upon their successful college teaching. As people who value education highly, they have been and continue to be very sensitive to educational experiences. They flourished under positive and benign experiences. Negative experiences caused them to make consequential choices. For example, some of their negative classroom experiences as students caused them to be very sensitive to the needs of their students and not to teach in ways that had negatively affected them. And conversely, as might be expected, they incorporated methods that resulted in positive classroom experiences into their own teaching.

Encouragement, love, and support from families who highly valued education existed in each participant's childhood. This support was given unconditionally and was not directed at pushing the participants toward any specific academic discipline. All the families provided literate environments in which the participants were encouraged to read and were read to as young children.

Only one of the parents had earned a doctorate. The others did not have as much education as their sons and daughters; yet they all valued education. All but one parent actively supported their children's education.

The socioeconomic backgrounds of the families varied from quite poor to upper middle class. It appears that the strong caring family values were much more important than their economic assets.

Traditional cultural values appear to be especially strong for two of the three minority persons in this study. Fred, a Native American from a Rio Grande Pueblo, and Fabi, a Chicana from the south valley of Albuquerque, highly value their cultures. They presently live and are raising their children in their native communities.

The female and male professors participating in this study all found it difficult to balance the different parts of their professional lives and maintain the level of achievement that they demand of themselves. They also found it difficult to balance their personal lives with their careers. There are not enough hours in the day for them to do all the things that they want to do.

The female mathematicians in my study are different from those in other research studies such as Becker's and Helson's. They are as confident mathematically and equally comfortable in social situations as the men in this study. The old stereotype of the socially inept, awkward, unattractive and unconfident female mathematician described in Helson's (1967) study was not supported in this study. In addition, all the women and men in this study embrace equitable values which support the development of all persons regardless of gender and ethnicity.

In contrast with previous studies, this group of individuals attended universities at a time when more opportunities were available for women and reflect the possibility of a cultural change. The average age for the participants in this study is 40 years while the average for eleven of the twelve is only 38.5 years. One participant was significantly older than the others. She attended graduate school after raising her family.

A qualitative study can identify transition points in a person's life. And although most of the women in this study had positive experiences with mathematics, one case illustrates the extraordinary impact of a negative educational experience.

The participants all emphasized the value of hard work. They attributed their 'modest' successes more to hard work and persistence than to their abilities. Obviously, both effort and ability were essential for their success in the academic world.

ACKNOWLEDGEMENT

I would like to acknowledge the contributions of Reuben Hersh, Vera John-Steiner, Breda Bova, and Kathryn Brooks to this research project.

BIBLIOGRAPHY

Becker, J.R. (1984) The pursuit of graduate education in mathematics: factors that influence women and men. *Journal of Educational Equity*, 4, 39–53.
Fennema, E. (1981) *Mathematical Education Research: Implications for the 80's*. Alexandria, VA: Association for Supervision and Curriculum Development.
Fennema, E. (1987, February) *Females and Mathematics*. Talk presented at the University of New Mexico.
Fennema, E. and Sherman, J. (1978) Sex-related differences in mathematics achievement and related factors: a further study. *Journal for Research in Mathematics Education*, 9, 189–203.
Gilligan, C. (1982) *In a Different Voice*. Cambridge, MA: Harvard University Press.
Halmos, P.R. (1985) *I Want to Be a Mathematician, An Automathography*. New York: Springer-Verlag.
Helson, R. (1967) Sex differences in creative style. *Journal of Personality*, 35, 214–33.
Helson, R. (1971) Women mathematicians and the creative personality. *Journal of Counseling and Clinical Psychology*, 34, 210–20.
National Council of Teachers of Mathematics Curriculum Standards for School Mathematics (1989) Reston, VA: National Council of Teachers of Mathematics.
Pedro, J.D., Wolleat, P., Fennema, E., and Becker, A.D. (1981) Election of high school mathematics by females and males: attributions and attitudes. *American Educational Research Journal*, 18, 207–18.
Rabi, I.I. (1987, June) Personal interview.
Reyes, L.H. (1984) Affective variables and mathematics education. *Elementary School Journal*, 54, 558–81.

Steen, L.A. (1987) Mathematics education: a predictor of scientific competitiveness. *Science*, **237**, 251–2, 302.

Taylor, L. (1988) *A Phenomenological Study of Female and Male University Professors' Life Histories in and Attitudes toward Mathematics*. Doctoral dissertation, University of New Mexico.

Chapter 6

Curriculum Development and Gender

Heleen Verhage

In this chapter, I would like to examine curriculum development for mathematics education and related research. Furthermore, I will pay particular attention in this matter to
the issue of gender. The perspective from which I shall discuss this subject is determined,
on the one hand, by a major innovative project in mathematics education in The Netherlands and, on the other hand, by the extensive work that has been done—and continues
to be done—by the work group 'Vrouwen en Wiskunde' (Women and Mathematics). I,
myself, am involved in both of the above-mentioned projects.

THE 12–16 MATHEMATICS PROJECT (W12–16)

The Dutch Secretary of Education established a committee in 1987 and assigned it the
task of developing a new mathematics programme for 12- to 16-year-olds. In 1992 this
committee must be ready to present its proposal for a new programme. The objective is
to develop and test this new programme in a number of schools.

Exams in The Netherlands are centralized and are therefore the same throughout the
country for all students from a given type of school. Students who, after elementary
school, attend a four-year high school (whether vocational or general secondary) will
take their final exam at the age of 16. In addition, there are five-year and six-year high
schools for, respectively, general secondary and college preparatory education. The
committee's task is, therefore, also to develop an exam programme for the four-year
schools. For some students, this exam functions at the same time as the entrance test for
further education, for others it marks the end of their school years. Both functions must
be taken into account in developing the new exam programme. At the moment, there are
two required subjects on the final exam (Dutch and one modern foreign language). For
the rest, the students may choose which subjects they wish to be examined on. As is the
case in so many other countries, fewer girls than boys choose mathematics.

In The Netherlands we are fortunate to have a woman as Secretary of Education who
sees emancipation as a major issue. As far as is in her power, she takes measures to
increase the participation of girls in maths and science. She has assigned the committee

the task of making sure that the programme will also be attractive to girls and that it will provide girls, too, with a favourable perspective in the job market. Explicit mention of this aspect in the assignment is a positive sign but, of course, much still remains to be done.

The actual work of developing a new mathematics programme is being carried out by a team of which I am a member. Approximately one-fourth of the team members are women—a fairly large proportion by Dutch standards, where women make up about 15 per cent of the mathematics teachers. If we view the increasing percentages of female students in teacher training courses, we can expect a gradual improvement in this situation. Unfortunately, this increasing number of women goes hand in hand with the diminishing status and deteriorating labour conditions in the teaching profession in The Netherlands.

The W12–16 project is unusually extensive and complex, as it must encompass mathematics education for *all* 12–16-year-old students. There are some 2500 secondary schools in The Netherlands, which provide work for more than 10,000 maths teachers. These teachers will in the future all need to be retrained. The project team has until 1992 to develop the new programme, alternating between desk work and putting the programme into practice at a number of test schools.

A VIEW OF MATHEMATICS EDUCATION

Which view of mathematics education lies at the base of the W12–16 project? In order to say anything on this subject, we must look at which trends in mathematics education are to be found in The Netherlands.

In my country there is a great deal of talk about so-called *realistic mathematics education*. By this is meant, among other things, that the mathematics taught must be derived from the reality around us and also be applicable to this reality. Realistic situations (indicated by context problems) are thus used as source and as area of application for mathematics education. The study group Vrouwen en Wiskunde has reflected on what this major role designated for contexts entails for girls. More of this later.

Another important characteristic of realistic mathematics education concerns *how* maths can be learned. Hans Freudenthal has stated that maths is a human activity and that one learns it by doing it. Students should, as it were, rediscover (scraps of) mathematics and construct it themselves. In this statement can be heard a specific viewpoint on the teaching and learning of mathematics. The task of the W12–16 project is to crystallize the ideas on realistic mathematics education into a curriculum. A similar project for the upper grades (16 +) has already been developed and has led to complete implementation of a new exam programme.

DEVELOPMENT RESEARCH

Curriculum development is part desk work, part field work. In ideal situations there is close collaboration with one or more test schools, where new pieces of subject matter and already outlined larger sections can be tried out. The curriculum to be developed must, of course, be legitimated, and the way in which this takes place must be explicitly demonstrated. The choice of subject matter is not determined beforehand but rather must take shape during the course of the project. In order to be able to do this well, the developers must continually reflect on their own work and demonstrate explicitly why certain choices have been made. Development work, therefore, contains in this sense a research component, which is why we speak in this context of *development research* (Gravemeijer).

During the experimentation, implicit ideas on what good mathematics education is are elaborated upon further. The developer continually reflects on the development work and on the experiences with the developed products and ideas. These reflections are helpful to the development work, the developer and the building of theories. In this way, implicit didactic ideas can gradually develop into more explicit theories.

CURRICULUM DEVELOPMENT IN PRACTICE: AN EXAMPLE

The W12–16 project is, therefore, working on a new mathematics curriculum which is based on a viewpoint designated by realistic mathematics education and according to the method of development research.

How this takes place in practice I shall now illustrate by means of a detailed example. In the case study which follows, I shall describe how my colleague, Marja Meeder, and I worked on developing learning materials on symmetry. We chose this subject under the assumption that it would appeal to many girls. A part of the internal report on our work (Meeder and Verhage) will be reproduced here.

At the beginning of February we came up with the idea of creating something together, having in mind the particular situation of female students and immigrants. We brainstormed on possible subjects and soon had a long list:

- Islamathematics
- Tangram
- symmetry in vignettes
- the golden section
- use of various grids
- anamorphoses
- cross-stitch, lace, patchwork, samplers
- tessellations
- computer drawings, fractals
- M.C. Escher
- Celtic patterns, meanders
- impossible figures
- wallpaper
- stamps
- garden tiles
- folding and cutting paper
- crockery

Considerations

What these subjects have in common is that they all contain cultural elements, appeal to an aesthetic sense, are visual and have to do with looking.

We chose symmetry because of the direct availability of material. We had in mind the symmetry of regular borders and tessellations. Upon browsing through the available textbooks it soon became clear that not much had been done on this subject and, where at all, it was on the symmetry of objects: zero-dimensional symmetry. Not, however, on the symmetry of edges, planes or in space. We started collecting material. In February we made a timetable and formulated some initial considerations. The most important were:

- The disadvantageous situation of girls and of immigrants in mathematics education should not only be investigated through already existing materials. New materials must be developed which especially appeal to these groups.
- In our own experience, making something oneself stimulates creativity, which leads to the discovery of new sources for mathematics education.
- It is inviting to lay links between mathematics and subjects other than the usual ones, for instance history, drawing, textiles.

At the end of February we rounded off the collection phase with a visit to the Museum of the Tropics.

We found our choice of subject matter confirmed in the book *Contemporary Mathematics* (COMAP, 1988). A number of things in this book appealed to us, such as the choice of subject matter and the informative bits of text which are entertaining to read. In our considerations we, of course, made use of a certain referential framework, for instance, the list of criteria put together by the Advisory Board on Learning Materials. In the criteria for science, it states that one must try to form a relation with:

- daily life
- society
- the professional world
- people and the human body
- historical development

We supplemented this with:

- other cultures (or would *cultural domains* be a better term?)

The learning materials

At the beginning of March we put the worksheets together. We divided them into *borders* and *tessellations* and decided to develop the border idea first. Borders would be for 13–14-year-olds and tessellations for 15–16-year-olds.

There were many things to be considered where the subject matter was concerned:

- do we address the students as 'you' singular or 'you' plural?
- how much cutting, pasting and busy-work do we include?

- what is the objective? Are there other objectives as well?
- what terminology do we use?
- how open, how directive should we be?
- what do we put in the teachers' guide?

Around the middle of March came the actual production of the material: hours sitting in front of the Macintosh computer and plenty of cutting, pasting and photocopying. At the end of March the first version was discussed at a team conference. Preparations for this conference brought forth two new ideas. The most important one is a variation on the so-called *tea-bag model*; vertical: extracts for lower school-types; horizontal: extracts for different target groups.

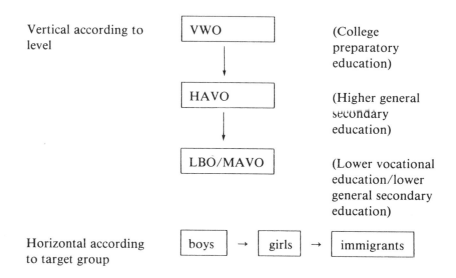

Observation: the embroidery project

At the beginning of June we brought the material into the classroom. The teacher had had a new idea of his own: let the class all embroider borders. He ordered materials (cardboard embroidery cards, needles, cotton thread) and we discussed together the making of worksheets to accompany the embroidery. The first assignment was 'Which front and reverse sides belong together?' (Figure 6.1).

The teacher had got the class so excited about embroidery beforehand, that the students entered the classroom the first day asking, 'Are we going to embroider today?' So when we did get around to embroidery during the fourth symmetry lesson, it didn't take much to get all the students busy embroidering.

The commentary was quite something:

Teacher:	Some of you can maybe figure out the first problem in your head, but we're going to actually do it first anyway.
Boy:	I don't get it at all.

Front side   *Reverse side*

1. basting stitch   a.

2. stem stitch   b.

3. back stitch   c.

4. satin stitch   d.

5. herringbone stitch   e.

6. buttonhole stitch   f.

Fig 6.1

Teacher:	Don't you know how to embroider?
Boy:	No.
Teacher:	Ask one of the girls.
Girl:	Now we just need cookies and a cup of tea.
Boy:	I'll do it in my head.
Teacher:	No, first you have to really do it yourself.
Boy:	This is the first time I've embroidered in my life.
Girl:	Teacher, do we also have to fasten off?
Boy:	What's that, 'fasten off'?
Boy:	Can I tear it out? Otherwise I have to thread the needle again.

Boy:	Teacher, how do you do the back stitch?
Teacher (to a girl):	M, how do you do the back stitch?
Girl:	Teacher, when are we going to knit?
Girl:	When his wife gets pregnant.
Girl:	I'm not so good at baby clothes—front panels and back panels and stuff.
Boy:	When do we learn to cook?
Girl:	This isn't math.
Teacher:	Why not?
Girl:	This is sewing class.
Teacher:	When you have to draw a circle you don't call it drawing class, do you?
Girl:	This is fun.
Boy:	I forgot my reading glasses.
Boy:	How do you do the back stitch?
Teacher (to a girl):	A, come explain the back stitch.
Girl:	What do we do if we're finished?
Teacher:	Are you finished already?
Boy:	Show-off.
Teacher:	Finish the stencil.
Boy:	They're just like bookmarks.
Teacher:	This has to be finished by next time. So it's homework.
Boy:	Homework?!
Teacher:	If you're smart, you'll ask your mother.
Boy:	Or my little sister.
Girl:	I'm going to call your mother and tell her that she and your little sister better not do it for you.
Boy:	Will we be tested on this?
Girl:	Let the boys flunk for once.
Girl:	How do you do the last one—the buttonhole stitch?
Boy:	The girls luck out, they've got easy homework.
Boy:	This is sure weird, embroidering during math class.
Teacher (to a girl):	You didn't fasten off, you just tied a knot.
Girl:	Yeah, but when you fasten off you mess up the other side.

Notwithstanding the comments, the students all did their best. After class I told the teacher that it was my impression that the girls clearly felt stronger during this lesson. They were at an advantage right away as it took many boys a while actually to get started due, for instance, to having trouble threading the needle. The teacher told how, during the previous lesson concerned with building brick walls, it had been just the other way around. The girls had had trouble determining from the frontal view just how the bricks had been laid. It worked out well that, in two successive lessons, first the boys and then the girls were at such a clear advantage.

The teacher told how he had asked two girls who are rather weak at maths to explain the back stitch to the boys. As a rule, these girls never have the chance to explain anything in maths class to someone else. Their self-confidence in maths is probably poor.

Among the other maths teachers (all men), the embroidery experiment was a much-discussed topic. Some of the comments I noted were:

Colleague: How did you get the idea? And find the material?
Teacher: Through my wife.
Colleague: Soon your wife will be teaching math here.
Other colleague: Can't you let the experiment be a flop? Otherwise next year I'll have
                    to embroider, too, and I'm not so crazy about that idea.

One thing is certain, the embroidery experiment created quite a stir at this school, among the teachers as well as the students. A pleasant aspect is that the idea did not come from us, the project co-ordinators, but from the teacher who was preparing a series of experimental lessons on border symmetry.

DISCUSSION

I have attempted here to provide an impression of our work in the W12–16 project and of the manner in which we have devoted attention to linking girls and mathematics. The project has, in fact, barely started and it is therefore much too early to draw final conclusions. Our goal is rather to reach what we call in the project *middle-level statements*. That is to say, statements on mathematics education that are, to a certain extent, generally valid and that have a solid basis, both in theory and in practice. Take, for instance, recommendations and guidelines for textbook authors, teachers, teacher-trainers and teachers of further education. In the course of the project, it must become clear exactly what we mean by 'mathematics education that appeals to girls'. The case study on the theme of symmetry presented above is the first attempt in the W12–16 project to arrive at general statements according to the principle of development research.

In what now follows I would like to elaborate further on certain matters which already have been mentioned in the example given. I will make use here of discussions that have taken place both in the work group Vrouwen en Wiskunde and elsewhere. The points raised are:

- the use of contexts
- aspects of emancipation in school textbooks
- the image of mathematics

Although I will deal with each point separately, they are certainly interconnected.

Use of contexts

As mentioned earlier, contexts play an important role in realistic mathematics education. The work group Vrouwen en Wiskunde has considered the question of what this entails for girls. It goes without saying that we must make use of contexts that girls find appealing. We then immediately run into the question of which contexts these should be. Should they be contexts that are derived from women's traditional domain—cooking, sewing and knitting, for instance? This is the point in the discussion where confusion arises. Are we involved here in emancipation or, on the contrary, are we busy confirming the traditional role patterns? Those who believe the latter will argue that use of recipes in maths class reconfirms stereotypes. What is the difference between this and the traditional pedagogy in which it was assumed that girls should be prepared for the household tasks and motherly duties awaiting them?

And yet I am still of the opinion that contexts such as cooking and sewing can be very useful in mathematics education, but then for boys as well as for girls, and for other reasons than the ones mentioned above. My arguments are the following:

- *A great deal of good mathematics can be found in these subjects.* For this reason alone it would be a pity not to make use of them. The problem, however, is that the majority of textbook authors, curriculum developers and teachers are men who, in general, are rather unfamiliar with these topics. One is often led by one's own preferences and hobbies. This is hardly surprising, but it does lead to systematic distortion and restriction of context choice. Mathematics education can be enriched by cultivating the fallow ground of women's traditional domain.
- *Bias in the choice of contexts leads systematically to putting groups of students at a disadvantage.* Particularly when introducing a new mathematics subject, a context should be chosen very carefully. After all, every true context requires the students' empathy. Those students who are already familiar with a given context therefore have the advantage over students for whom the context is less familiar, or perhaps entirely new. By the time 12-year-olds reach high school, the socialization process in which they have been formed to behave as boys and girls has to a great extent already taken place. One of the effects here is that boys and girls will have different foreknowledge regarding contexts. So we cannot avoid the fact that girls will empathize less than boys with contexts chosen from the male world of interests.
- *Mathematics education can contribute to the emancipation of both girls and boys.* Mathematics that is rich in contexts automatically contains many subjects from the male cultural domain. This is, on the one hand, due to the close ties between maths, the sciences and technology and, on the other hand, due to the textbook authors' backgrounds. One aspect of emancipation is to awaken girls' interest in maths and science and in the professional world surrounding it. But the complement of this is to help boys become familiar with topics from the female cultural domain. And these topics are not automatically found in mathematics education. To restore the balance, extra attention must therefore be paid here.

Research into aspects of emancipation in school textbooks

A recent research project in The Netherlands dealt with aspects of emancipation in school textbooks (Mottier, 1988). The criteria mentioned in the above case study for learning materials that break through role patterns are based on this. The following three aspects of emancipation are distinguished in this research:

- breaking through role limitation: offering a wide range of roles to women and men
- making up the arrears: discontinuing women's invisibility
- providing equal opportunity to identify with the subject matter: offering both boys and girls motivating subject matter

The reasoning here is that, if all these aspects are well taken into account by the textbooks, it will have a positive effect on girls' educational chances.

The first two aspects have primarily to do with stereotypes in language use and illustrations. Men and women are portrayed in stereotyped roles and women hardly ever appear in the text or in illustrations. Through the years, research in various countries has pointed out and denounced this situation. I myself am, of course, of the opinion that every author should take care not to portray men and women in a stereotyped fashion. But, in a certain sense, I find the third aspect more intriguing, as it goes deeper than language use alone. '. . . opportunity to identify with the subject matter' is elaborated upon further in this research project:

- attention to the varying interests of boys and girls, and inclusion of the interests of both groups in the subject matter
- attention to the past of men and women, that is, to their history
- attention to the present position of men and women, their social roles, their various activities and characteristics, the unequal recognition of male and female values
- attention to the perspective for boys and girls, choice of profession, professional image, career perspectives, double-role expectations

The next step in the research was to draw up guidelines based on this for school textbooks. The third aspect—identification with the subject matter—was here elaborated upon for various subjects. The specific criteria for the sciences were already mentioned above in the case study and are as follows:

- daily life
- society
- the professional world
- people and the human body
- historical development

I call attention in this paper to the research described above because, in my opinion, these criteria can give us something to go on in our work. The fact that the criteria were developed in the first place for physics and not for maths in no way detracts from their applicability. It appeals to me that they extend further than simply counting word frequencies (he/she, etc.) and are connected closely with the discussion on contexts in the previous section. These criteria for mathematics should be crystallized further within the framework of the W12–16 project and the viewpoint outlined above on realistic mathematics education.

The image of mathematics

In an innovative project such as W12–16, one is constantly confronted with the image people (teachers, students, parents) have of mathematics. Everyone has, as a matter of fact, a certain image of maths, without necessarily knowing much about the subject. This discussion on 'the image of mathematics' is carried on in various places and from various points of view. One of these places is the work group Vrouwen en Wiskunde, in which we were inspired, among other things, by a lecture given by Leone Burton in our country in the Spring of 1987. This lecture has been incorporated in the book *Vriendelijke Wiskunde* (Friendly Mathematics), from which I have taken the following characterizations of mathematics (Meeder *et al.*, 1987).

Mathematics is often seen as something abstract, objective, logical, true, well-defined and certain. I would like to call this the *static image* of mathematics. When mathematics education is presented which does not fit this image, the question immediately arises 'but is that maths?' The new must prove itself in relation to the old, which derives its status from the unquestionability of tradition, and then primarily the tradition of mathematics as a science.

Opposing the static image of formal mathematics, we can easily place something quite different:

- mathematics generalizes, attempts to find connections; this need not be abstract
- mathematics can also be subjective
- mathematics is in search of internal consistency
- mathematics does not hold the one absolute truth; mathematics is relative
- mathematics is not intrinsically, and as a matter of course, well-defined
- mathematics can also present itself questioningly and searchingly

Mathematics is not, in the first place, a copy-cat subject, but rather a creative one. In this way maths can become something personal, something of one's own. I call this the *dynamic image* of mathematics. In her book *Reflections on Gender and Science*, Evelyn Fox Keller (1985) attempts to explain how the static image (she speaks of the 'male character') of the sciences came into being and still persists. We have paid this much attention to 'the distorted image of mathematics' in the work group Vrouwen en Wiskunde because we believe that what I call here the dynamic image of mathematics will particularly appeal to women and girls.

IN CONCLUSION

In this contribution I have attempted to say something about the mathematics curriculum and its development in The Netherlands. My referential framework was formed by the important innovative project W12–16 in which I am involved. I consider it a challenge during the course of this project to try and connect the views behind realistic mathematics education with ideas on the image of mathematics, in theory as well as in practice. Where the practical work of curriculum development is concerned, it is important that the contexts for mathematics problems be chosen with care. The criteria for aspects of emancipation in school textbooks can perhaps offer some support here. There are, of course, many other factors than the content of the mathematics curriculum which influence girls' participation in mathematics education.

ACKNOWLEDGEMENT

Many of the ideas contained in this chapter took shape during our discussions in the work group Vrouwen en Wiskunde. I am grateful to have been able to make use of them on this occasion.

BIBLIOGRAPHY

Burton, L. (1987) Women and mathematics: is there an intersection? (abbreviated version) *IOWME Newsletter*, **3** (1).

Consortium for Mathematics and Its Applications (COMAP) (1988) *Introduction to Contemporary Mathematics*, L. A. Steen (ed.), New York: W. H. Freeman.

Freudenthal, H. (1973) *Mathematics as an Educational Task*. Utrecht: Reidel.

Gravemeijer, K. Internal report on development research.

Keller, E. Fox (1985) *Reflections on Gender and Science*. New Haven: Yale University Press.

Meeder, M., Meester, F., Verhage, H. and Eenbergen, S. van (1987) *Vriendelijke Wiskunde*. Amsterdam: Werkgroep Vrouwen en Wiskunde.

Meeder, M. and Verhage, H. Internal report on 'Op de Rand'.

Mottier, I. (1988) *Emancipatieaspecten in schoolboeken*. Dissertation, University of Leiden.

Chapter 7

Humanizing Calculus: A Case Study in Curriculum Development

Mary Barnes and Mary Coupland

This chapter reports the planning and development of a short introductory calculus course for adult students, offered as part of the University of Sydney's Continuing Education Programme. The main objective of the course was to give people in the wider community outside the university a chance to learn about some of the powerful ideas that have influenced the development of present-day mathematics and science. But the two women who planned and taught the course had a second objective: to encourage women's interest in mathematics, to build up their confidence and to increase their opportunities to study it further.

In Australia, many students receive an introduction to differential and integral calculus during their final two years of high school, and a wide range of university and college programmes assume that entering students have taken such a course. Lack of any knowledge of calculus therefore constitutes a serious handicap for adults wanting to return to study and for school leavers who did not make appropriate choices in high school. The lower participation of women in mathematics, especially in the past, means that women form a majority of those disadvantaged in this way. The Mathematics Learning Centre had received a number of enquiries from people who wanted to learn a little about calculus and its applications. The course we offered was intended as a short introduction to the ideas and methods of calculus rather than a rigorous grounding in the subject.

WHAT MAKES CALCULUS DIFFICULT?

From informal discussions with adult students, we were aware that many people perceived calculus as difficult, and that many of those who had taken a course in calculus felt that they had never really understood what it was all about. So when we sat down to plan our course we began by thinking about possible reasons for these attitudes.

The first problem we identified was lack of motivation. People we talked to who had done some calculus had a very restricted view of its potential applications. A survey of introductory calculus texts helps to explain this: no applications to the real world are presented, or even hinted at, in the initial stages. Applications are left till later—for those who persevere long enough. The usual introduction to calculus is completely abstract: the problem posed is how to find the gradient of the tangent to a curve, and no indication is given of why this might be important or interesting. The first applications presented are usually described as 'applications to geometry' and consist of curve sketching—yet another totally abstract activity, fascinating to mathematicians but unmotivating for most other people unless it is presented in some relevant context. Next come 'practical' problems of maximizing or minimizing some quantity, but many of these are patently artificial, often so over-simplified that they are meaningless. Others are business oriented—what selling price of goods will produce the maximum profit, what shape of packaging will use the least materials? Lastly there are 'applications to the physical world', which are mainly problems about projectiles, including bullets, cannonballs and rockets. Those who progress further may learn about stretched springs, systems of pulleys and even pile-drivers. Students may conclude from this that calculus is primarily highly abstract pure mathematics. Those uses that are presented in introductory courses can be summarized as profits, weapons and machines.

Another problem is caused by the conceptual difficulty of the introductory stages. Calculus usually begins with a discussion of limits. In spite of all our efforts to keep it as simple as possible, this leaves many students bewildered. The definition of a limit requires considerable mathematical sophistication before it can be properly understood, so a formal treatment of limits is not appropriate for most beginning students. But if we talk about limits only in informal terms, we tend to gloss over the difficulties and, as a result, students cannot see the point of it all. After limits comes 'differentiation from first principles', which not only involves the limit concept, but uses unfamiliar notation and frequently requires quite complicated algebraic manipulations. When students finally learn that differentiation can be reduced to a fairly simple list of rules which can be applied mechanically, they are usually very relieved and often decide to ignore everything that went before, and simply memorize the rules. As one student observed, 'It's just like teachers to show you the hard way first, and not tell you there's an easy way until afterwards'. The result of the usual approach to beginning calculus, therefore, is that many students give up trying to understand, and resort to instrumental learning, their only purpose being to get through an examination and then forget it all.

WHAT ARE THE PARTICULAR BARRIERS FOR WOMEN?

The preceding discussion helps to explain why many people drop out of, or lose interest in, calculus courses. However, since we wanted to pay particular attention to the needs and interests of women and ways of encouraging their participation in the course, we turned to the literature on women and mathematics.

If we survey the results of research in this area, we find one constantly recurring observation: many more women than men see mathematics as neither relevant to their interests and experiences nor useful to them in their future lives and careers (see e.g. Fennema, 1979; Brush, 1985; Chipman and Wilson, 1985; Eccles *et al.*, 1985; Open University, 1987).

This may apply particularly to calculus, as the preceding analysis of course content indicates. The uses of calculus presented are all associated with activities which in our present society are stereotyped as male. The overall impression which students might gain is that calculus helps to provide *man* with power to control his world, by means of weapons, machines and self-interested economic decision-making. It should not be surprising that many women find this irrelevant to their concerns, or that a traditional calculus course may tend to reinforce the idea, so frequently presented in the media, that mathematics is a male domain.

The teaching methods used in mathematics can also create barriers to women's participation. We know that women express much less preference than men for competitive or individualistic approaches to learning and a greater preference for a co-operative mode (Owens, 1981). The traditional style of mathematics teaching is authoritarian and teacher-centred, and tends to encourage a competitive atmosphere. The confident, assertive student thrives in such a classroom, while the more reticent and less confident are disadvantaged. There is an abundance of research results showing that women are more likely to come into the latter category.

MOTIVATING CALCULUS

It was against this background that we set about planning the course. We wanted to focus on increasing motivation, building confidence, developing teaching methods to suit women's learning styles as well as men's and avoiding the creation of conceptual difficulties. The course would need to deal with applications to issues of interest to women, and avoid relying on scientific and technical knowledge with which men in our society might be more familiar. But what sort of topics would be appropriate?

To answer this question we turned to feminist critiques of psychological theory and science education which we felt might also be relevant to mathematics education. The work of Gilligan (1982), for example, drew attention to differences in the ways in which men and women develop their values and their sense of identity. Gilligan claims that while men define their identity in terms of autonomy and separation, that of women 'is defined in a context of relationships and judged by a standard of responsibility and care' (p. 160). Head (1985) draws similar conclusions from his own research and that of others. Harding (1987) has used these ideas in designing a chemistry course which introduces 'the hard stuff of chemistry' through social issues such as acid rain or the world food supply. This course was very successful with girls, because they felt that it justified the study of chemistry by showing why it was important.

We believed that a calculus course which introduced, in a similar way, issues of 'responsibility and care' would have similar success. It would certainly have more appeal for women than the traditional courses, which could be described as dealing with power and control. There are many present-day issues of importance to people concerned about the future of our planet and its population in which questions of growth and change are important. In most of these, mathematical models of the problem can be built, and calculus used to analyse, understand and predict outcomes. Such questions include: world population growth; populations of endangered species; disposal of radioactive waste; spread of an infectious disease through a population; the rate of absorption of a drug, or alcohol, into the bloodstream and the subsequent rate of elimination; and the build-up of pollutants in lakes and rivers. Of course, in many cases the technical details of a mathematical solution to the problem are rather too difficult to be treated fully in an introductory course. But we felt that this should not deter us from mentioning them as potential applications of the ideas and techniques we were studying, and introducing simplified models where possible.

Human interest was introduced into the course not only through these large themes. In many smaller ways too we tried to relate abstract ideas to everyday experience. Our discussion of exponential functions, for example, began by talking about family trees and then posing the question 'How would you work out how many great-great-great-great-grandparents you had?' Variations and extensions of this led us to the function $y = 2^x$ and eventually to $y = e^x$.

The sequencing of the course was planned so that the exponential function was introduced rather earlier than is usual. This allowed us to spend some time discussing questions of population growth and radioactive decay. Population growth is a particularly suitable topic for a course such as this, not only for political, ecological and humanitarian reasons, but also because of the number of different growth models that have been proposed, from the simple Malthusian model of exponential growth to a variety of 'limited growth' models. This provides opportunities to discuss the appropriateness of different models, and to dispel the idea that in mathematics there is just one right method and one right answer. The use of calculators and computers to help us in computation and graphing made the analysis of more realistic problems feasible.

Another matter of concern to us was the image of mathematics which many people hold—as absolute truth, rigorous and objective, and therefore culture free and value free. Burton (1986) has discussed the origins of this view of the discipline, and its transmission by means of traditional methods of teaching and assessment. Too frequently, mathematics is seen as remote and unchanging, all worked out long ago, and unrelated to human concerns. We know that for many women this perception has made mathematics hard to come to terms with. One of Buerk's (1985) subjects, for example, described it as being 'like a stainless steel wall—hard, cold, smooth, offering no handhold' and described how she resented its 'cold impenetrability'.

We believed that we could motivate students, especially women, by helping them to see calculus as a human creation, developed in a particular cultural and historical context, by mathematicians who were influenced by the needs and values of the society they lived in. And so we decided to incorporate some of the history of calculus into the course.

To give an illustration, we spent some time during the first class talking about why calculus was created at the time that it was. We discussed the kinds of problems that mathematicians like Newton and Leibniz were trying to solve, which led them to invent the calculus. But we also asked *why* these problems were thought to be important at that time. The students learned that all of these questions were related in some way to astronomy (Kline, 1972, pp. 342–3) and that astronomy was particularly important in that period because of the needs of navigators to find better ways of measuring their position accurately (Kline, 1972, pp. 336–7). Governments were even offering rich prizes for better solutions to the problem because accurate navigation was important for exploration, colonization and trade. Thus the development of calculus was influenced by the desires of some European nations to extend their wealth and power.

At a later stage we talked about the different notations used in calculus, and their origins. Students looked at examples of the notations used by Newton and Leibniz and we discussed the way a poor notation can make things seem confusing while a good one makes them easier to follow and can be helpful in solving problems.

TEACHING METHODOLOGY

Owens' research, reported earlier, suggested that the introduction of co-operative learning activities would benefit women students. This has been supported by Fennema and Peterson (1987, p. 124). Further support comes from research in science education which found that teachers who used student-centred enquiry methods were more effective than others in maintaining girls' liking for the subject (Eggleston *et al.*, 1976; quoted in Open University, 1987). Such methods involve co-operation among students, and by decreasing the amount of public interaction with the teacher provide less opportunity for a competitive spirit to develop. Furthermore, interacting with a small group during collaborative work allows women to make effective use of their verbal abilities in discussions which can help to clarify their ideas, and the small group setting provides a supportive environment which can help to boost self-confidence.

Just as traditional teacher-dominated methods perpetuate the formal view of mathematics, student-centred enquiry methods help students to understand the role of intuition, imagination and creativity and to recognize the importance of the process by which mathematics is derived (Burton, 1986). So we felt it important to incorporate these methods in our teaching. As far as possible, we aimed to make the course 'problem driven'. That is, instead of beginning by teaching an abstract technique, allowing students to practise it and then giving them some problems to which it could be applied, we began with a problem, allowed students to investigate possible ways of solving it, encouraged them to discuss and compare different methods, and through further investigation and discussion gradually developed the theory and techniques.

We also wanted to change the power structure of the classroom to give students more control over their own learning. This meant encouraging them to express their wishes about course content and methods and then negotiating the curriculum with them (see Boomer, 1982). At the beginning of the first session we asked the students to discuss in small groups their reasons for taking the course and what they hoped to gain from it. Each group then reported back to the whole class and this was followed by general discussion on the goals of the course. We then asked them, again in small groups, to spend a little time sharing with one another what they thought calculus was about and what it was useful for. By moving around and listening to different groups the teachers were able to gain useful information about students' prior knowledge and misconceptions. This was useful in determining the level at which to begin and the ideas to emphasize. This process of negotiation initially resulted in some conflict between our ideas and what the students wanted. For example, we would have liked everyone to take part in small group activities, but one or two students preferred to work alone. We explained why we felt that working in a group was a good idea, but if they still did not want to join in, we left them to work in the way they preferred.

In the end, because of the diversity of student backgrounds and needs, we adopted a variety of different teaching methods. We used lecturettes to introduce new topics and to convey historical information; small group investigations to let students explore new ideas and experiment with different methods of solving problems; and both small group and whole class discussions to help students to clarify their thoughts, express concepts in their own words, and so consolidate their understanding.

AVOIDING CONCEPTUAL DIFFICULTIES

We felt that it was important, in an introductory course, to avoid discussion of limits and differentiation from first principles because of the difficulty they cause. But we wanted students to develop a good understanding of the meaning of the derivative as a rate of change, and its geometrical interpretation as the slope of a graph. Computer graphics provided an invaluable tool to help us achieve this. The computer package we used (Tall, 1985a) was designed especially for this purpose. It has the facility to graph the 'gradient function' (i.e. the derivative) of a given function and then compare this graph with that of a conjectured formula for the derivative. Thus, students were encouraged to look for patterns in the results they obtained, formulate conjectures, test them, and if necessary modify the conjectures and test again. In this process, the use of the computer seemed to encourage conjecturing. A 'wrong' answer, displayed on the computer screen, becomes useful data to be used in working out a better suggestion; whereas a 'wrong' answer recorded in the student's notebook is more permanent and so seems to be more threatening to the self-esteem. This approach is described in more detail in Tall (1985b) and Barnes (1988).

Use of a computer in this way as a tool for investigative activities allowed us to treat calculus as an experimental subject. By working through carefully structured activities, students were helped to 'discover' many of the differentiation rules for themselves. The excitement they derived from making their own discoveries provided positive reinforcement for their learning. This encouraged them to go further, choose their own topics for investigation and pose their own problems.

On occasions we found it useful to introduce manipulative materials to help students come to grips with a problem and explore possibilities. For example, when introducing maxima and minima we began by posing a familiar problem: 'Mrs Jones, a keen gardener, wants to fence off a section of her backyard for a vegetable garden. She has 18 metres of fencing wire. What is the biggest rectangular area she can enclose?' Each group of students was given 18 matchsticks to represent the wire and asked to investigate possible shapes and sizes for the garden. They recorded the results of their investigations, mostly in the form of tables. At one stage we intervened to point out to some groups that the sides of the rectangle did not have to be whole numbers, and that it was permissible to break some of the matches into smaller pieces. When the groups had found an answer, we encouraged them to investigate further, to try to generalize and to look for alternative ways of representing their data. Someone suggested drawing a graph, and so we graphed the area of the rectangle against the length of one of its sides. We continued to pose further questions:

- Now we've got a graph. It represents a function. Can you work out a formula for it?
- Can you describe how this function changes as the length of the side gradually increases?
- In particular, where is the area increasing rapidly, where is it increasing slowly, and where does it begin to decrease?
- Finally, remembering that the derivative of a function is its rate of change, can you explain how we could use the derivative of the function to help us locate the maximum value?

After we had worked out a procedure for finding maximum values, we went on to explore variations on the problem and then to apply the same approach to new problems. Many of the students in the class had rather weak mathematical backgrounds. It was clear that the use of concrete aids in this way to help them visualize the problem not only enabled them to find a numerical answer, but also helped in deriving an expression for the function, and made the whole procedure more meaningful.

OUTCOMES

The course, consisting of eight 2-hour class meetings, was run for the first time from September to November, 1987, and attracted an enrolment of 24 students—the upper bound on class size which we had specified. We were a little disappointed to find that only about 40 per cent of the students were women, in contrast to some of the other Continuing Education courses offered by the Mathematics Learning Centre (Rediscovering Mathematics, Overcoming Maths Anxiety) in which women form a majority. Perhaps we should not have been surprised. This is just a reflection of the same pattern as has been observed in most western countries—the higher the level of mathematics, the lower the participation rate of women.

Unlike many adult education courses, this was not a recreational course requiring no commitment outside class time. If they were to achieve anything worthwhile in the short time available, students had to put in some effort and so we set regular homework each week. Like the classes, we tried to make the homework interesting, and to include a variety of real-life applications. Homework was often checked in groups, with students comparing solutions and helping one another, turning to the computer to verify the correctness of their graphs.

Of those enrolled, about half had taken a course in calculus previously, perhaps many years earlier, but felt they had not understood it properly. Many wanted to gain confidence before enrolling for further studies, often in business or commerce courses for which some familiarity with calculus would be assumed. The rest had never done calculus, and some had a very shaky understanding of elementary algebra. One student was concurrently attending a Higher School Certificate course at a technical college. His comment on the course was 'I learned the rules and procedures at Tech, but *this* course gave me far better insight into what it was all about'. This was typical of student reaction to the course. Those who attended, both female and male, expressed a high degree of satisfaction and enjoyment.

There were some problems, however, caused mainly by differences in students' prior knowledge and their preconceived ideas about how mathematics should be learned, which often conflicted with our ideas about how we wanted to teach it. At the beginning of the course, one mature age woman student was so shy and lacking in confidence that she refused to join in discussion with other students, even in a small group. This attitude changed with time, however. At first she simply sat and listened to the others. Later, she ventured some ideas of her own, and when these were accepted and valued by the group, and mentioned later in the whole-class discussion, she began to gain more confidence. This student had arrived at the first class carrying a yellowed book of logarithm tables—standard equipment for the mathematics student at the time when she last studied the subject! We taught her how to use a calculator, and then introduced her to the joys of microcomputer graphics. Perhaps the most memorable comment of the whole course came from this woman as she faced her first encounter with a computer, 'This is so exciting! I never knew mathematics could be like this.'

THE FUTURE

We plan to offer the course again in the latter part of 1988. Meanwhile we are planning another new course, Investigating Algebra and Graphs, which will serve as preparation for the calculus course. We hope that this will help people who are less confident about their mathematical skills to prepare for calculus. We will also need to think about advertising our courses through women's networks, instead of relying on the publicity arranged by the University's Centre for Continuing Education. In this way we may be able to get the message across to women that here is a course designed and taught by women, with women's needs and interests in mind, in which they have a greater chance of enjoying mathematics and experiencing success.

REFERENCES

Barnes, M.S. (1988) Teaching calculus with a micro computer—an investigative approach. In Pegg, J. (ed.) *Mathematical Interfaces*. Newcastle, Australia: Australian Association of Mathematics Teachers.

Boomer, G. (ed.) (1982) *Negotiating the Curriculum*. Sydney, Australia: Ashton Scholastic.

Brush, L. (1985) Cognitive and affective determinants of course preferences and plans. In Chipman, S.F., Brush, L.R. and Wilson, D.M. (eds) *Women and Mathematics: Balancing the Equation*. Hillsdale, NJ: Lawrence Erlbaum.

Buerk, D. (1985) The voices of women making meaning in mathematics. *Journal of Education*, 167, 59–70.

Burton, L. (1986) Femmes et mathématique: y a-t-il une intersection? In Lafortune, L. (ed.) *Femmes et Mathématique*. Montréal: Les Editions du Remue Ménage. (For an abbreviated English version see: Women and mathematics: is there an intersection? *IOWME Newsletter*, 3(1), 4–7.)

Chipman, S.F. and Wilson, D.M. (1985) Understanding mathematics course enrolment and mathematics achievement: a synthesis of the research. In Chipman, S.F., Brush, L.R. and Wilson, D.M. (eds) *Women and Mathematics: Balancing the Equation*. Hillsdale, NJ: Laurence Erlbaum.

Eccles, J., Adler, T.F., Futterman, R., Goff, S.B., Kaczala, C.M., Meece, J.L. and Midgley, C. (1985) Self-perceptions, task perceptions, socialising influences, and the decision to enroll in mathematics. In Chipman, S.F., Brush, L.R. and Wilson, D.M. (eds) *Women and Mathematics: Balancing the Equation*. Hillsdale, NJ: Lawrence Erlbaum.

Eggleston, J., Galton, M. and Jones, M. (1976) *Processes and Products of Science Teaching*. London: Schools Council Research Studies, Macmillan Education.

Fennema, E. (1979) Women and girls in mathematics: equity in mathematics education. *Educational Studies in Mathematics*, 10, 389–401.

Fennema, E. and Peterson, P. (1987) Effective teaching for girls and boys: The same or different? In Berliner, D.C. and Rosenshine, B.V. (eds) *Talks to Teachers*. New York: Random House.

Gilligan, C. (1982) *In a Different Voice*. Cambridge, MA: Harvard University Press.

Harding, J. (1987) Filtered out or opting in? *Education Links*, 32, 12–14.

Head, J. (1985) *The Personal Response to Science*. Cambridge: Cambridge University Press.

Kline, M. (1972) *Mathematical Thought from Ancient to Modern Times*. New York: Oxford University Press.

Open University (1987) *Girls into Mathematics*. Cambridge: Cambridge University Press.

Owens, L. (1981) The cooperative, competitive, and individualised learning preference of primary and secondary teachers in Sydney. In *Proceedings of the Annual Conference of the Australian Association for Research in Education*, Vol. 1, pp. 142–150.

Tall, D. (1985a) *Graphic Calculus I* and *Supergraph*. London: Glentop.

Tall, D. (1985b) Understanding the calculus. *Mathematics Teaching*, **110**, 49–53.

Chapter 8

Women and Maths in Australia: A Confidence-building Experience for Teachers and Students

Beth Marr and Sue Helme

The extent of gender segmentation in Australia's workforce is amongst the worst in the world. The majority of women are confined to three occupations: clerk, salesperson and stenographer/typist, all of which are low-paid and low-status.

Consequently, women are found in very low numbers in technical or scientific jobs, for which maths and physical science are basic prerequisites. For example, women comprise less than one per cent of skilled tradespeople, 16 per cent of technicians and 7 per cent of engineers or applied scientists (Dillon, 1986). The picture for education is similar, in that the bulk of women's enrolment is concentrated in a narrow field of non-technical courses.

The under-participation of girls and women in maths and science is well documented, as are the historical, cultural and educational forces which combine to discourage women from continuing with these subjects. The attitude that 'girls don't need maths' has resulted in large numbers of adult women who, having failed at maths in the past, have very little confidence in their ability. This attitude is often conveyed to their daughters, thus perpetuating the cycle. Even today, girls at school continue to select subjects with a primarily humanities or commercial bias, to the exclusion of maths and science.

MAKING CHANGES

In the last five or six years government policy-makers have been forced to recognize this as a problem and have begun to put money into schemes encouraging women and girls into maths/science areas. In secondary education the schemes are aimed at encouraging girls to retain maths and science at higher levels. They are experimenting with segregated classes and changes in content and delivery more suited to the learning styles of young female students. In TAFE (Technical and Further Education) we have been tackling the problems from a different angle by attempting to attract adult women back to education in the maths/science arena.

Women teachers and Equal Opportunity Officers in the TAFE system have worked within their individual colleges to set up a variety of 'bridging' programmes. These differ in length but are usually six months or a year, some full-time and some part-time. A bridging programme aims to take participants without mathematical skills to a stage where they have the prerequisites and confidence to enter vocational training courses or advanced education.

Mathematics courses for women are also conducted in community houses and neighbourhood learning centres, non-threatening environments which offer childcare and run weekly classes.

THE ADULT WOMAN STUDENT

A typical student in such a course would have completed less than three years of secondary education mathematics, and left school with very little mathematical competence. She may have a definite career goal in mind, such as a vocational course, but is more likely to be uncertain about her capabilities, interests and goals. This course is a first, often tentative, step back into education and career decision-making.

Her experience of maths in secondary school was likely to have been of years of sitting in class understanding little of what was said by a remote and impatient teacher who ignored her in favour of high-achieving students. She would have been alienated by the textbook examples which used male-oriented activities to solve problems that had very little to do with her life and experiences. Moreover, traditional classroom organization—rows of students sitting quietly at desks—denied her the valuable opportunity of discussing problems with other students, reinforcing her feelings of isolation and fear, and contributing very little to her learning.

Returning to study is a major step, requiring a great deal of courage and determination: not only to overcome her fears about learning and uncertainties about her capabilities, but also to make the adjustments in her personal and family life necessary to accommodate her new role as a student. For this, a supportive and understanding learning environment is essential.

RESPONDING TO THE NEED

Aware that the male environment of the typical TAFE college can be alien and frightening to most adult women, teachers conducting women's or bridging courses within colleges have put special effort into making the students feel comfortable, by providing tea and coffee facilities, and creating a friendly atmosphere. We encourage them as much as possible to feel that they have a legitimate place in the college.

Once the courses got underway we soon realized that traditional materials and methods for teaching basic maths were inappropriate for adult women students. Although there were plenty of basic maths books for children or the aspiring young male technician, nothing reflecting the lives, needs and interests of adults—particularly women—was available. Teachers responded by developing resources and teaching methods which were more appropriate for adult learners.

As these courses grew in number, so did the need for communication, and interested women first came together at *Women Who Teach Women Maths and Science*, a conference held in December 1985. At this conference we shared many of the ideas and resources that had until then been developed in isolation. We also had the opportunity to experience some of the activities created by the EQUALS organization from the USA and the McClintock Collective, a group of women science teachers working on new methods of teaching science to girls in secondary schools. The conference generated enormous energy and enthusiasm, highlighting the importance of networking to share and develop ideas.

Soon after the conference we obtained national funding for The Teaching Maths to Women Project. Its aims were to develop appropriate teaching materials and techniques for adult learners, particularly women; to adapt such materials from overseas for the local scene and to provide staff development for other teachers in the use of these materials. A group of ten teachers from the original conference from both country and city venues worked together on this project and became a cohesive and supportive writing team. None of us was confident or experienced at writing or conducting staff development when we began.

We started by holding a series of workshops where we brainstormed our ideas on the topics we considered important to include, and how we would teach them. This was an exciting process as ideas bounced backwards and forwards, gaining momentum, sparking more ideas, and growing into new activities and exercises. Individuals in the group then wrote outlines for particular sections, and brought them back to the group for review and trialing with students. The results of this process were the development of our writing skills, our ability to give and receive constructive criticism of each others' ideas and work and, finally, the publication of *Mathematics: A New Beginning*.

OUR MATERIALS AND METHODS

We have developed what we believe are important criteria for the successful teaching—and learning—of mathematics and have attempted as much as possible to put these into practice in designing our publication. Most of these criteria apply to the teaching of mathematics to anyone—young, old, male, female—but are specially relevant to adult women returning to study.

Our materials and methods attempt to:

- ensure that all students in the group perform tasks at which they can experience *success*. This will build their confidence as they progress through their course.
- encourage students to learn through *interaction* and *co-operation*, which involve discussion, asking questions, explaining their reasoning to others, and working co-operatively in pairs or small groups.
- use *practical activities* and *hands-on materials*. Effective learning takes place when students start with their own experience and build on that experience to develop rules, which they can then apply in unfamiliar situations. Another advantage of hands-on materials is that students can return to them if they forget the process or wish to check their reasoning.
- teach concepts in a *context* relevant to adult students, drawing from their backgrounds, interests and experiences. This includes placing mathematical ideas in their historical and social framework.
- raise *awareness* about social and economic structures influencing our lives, particularly the lives of Australian women. This can be done by developing examples that

refer to data and information currently available in the press, government reports and from other media sources.

- acknowledge *differences* between students in their backgrounds and levels of mathematical skill, have the scope to be used at a variety of levels within a class and contain a range of reinforcing activities to be done at home or in subsequent sessions.

Content

To decide on the content of the book we asked ourselves the following questions: What do women *want* to learn? What do they *need* to learn in order to establish a firm base on which to build their mathematical skills and confidence? The end result was a collection of material that we organized into seven sections:

- *Getting Started* contains a selection of activities to generate a supportive classroom atmosphere and build students' confidence in their ability to learn mathematics.
- *Exploring Numbers* explores the historical basis of our decimal system, develops students' skills with whole numbers and decimals and introduces directed numbers
- *Fractions* uses a 'hands on' approach to teach fraction concepts and operations with fractions. It also includes sessions that focus on applying fraction skills to problem-solving situations.
- *Metrics and Measurement* is designed for students to whom the metric system is unfamiliar and often bewildering. Many practical activities are included that reinforce both the concepts and units used in measurement.
- *Estimation and Calculators* teaches students to use a calculator, which is for many a new and unfamiliar technological tool. Estimation skills are developed to build confidence in reading and understanding quantitative information as well as for checking the reasonableness of calculator results.
- *Problem-solving* develops students' skills in reading and understanding information, extracting the relevant material from problems expressed in words, and explores a number of strategies for solving such problems.
- *Fractions in Action: Ratios and Percentages* explores two of the applications of fractions that occur most frequently in everyday life.

More sections are planned for inclusion and are almost complete. Algebra and Graphs and Geometry will be available in the near future.

Format

To encourage as many people as possible to use the material, and to spread its use beyond the maths-trained (we were surprised by the number of literacy teachers attending our in-services) we adopted a highly structured format. The material is organized in Session Outlines, which are written in sufficient detail to be used successfully just as they are.

We were also concerned that the material should look appealing and easy to use, and took special care in its design. The outcome is a book that we believe is organized, clear, well-illustrated and visually uncluttered: something that teachers would *want* to pick up and use. The positive feedback we have received so far indicates that we have met our goals in this respect.

IN-SERVICING

Another important aim of the project was to develop the professional skills of teachers working with adults and so funds were allocated for this purpose.

We conducted several one-day in-service programmes and presented many workshops at other conferences in order to:

- try out our resources on other teachers, incorporate their ideas and feedback, and generate a receptive audience for our materials.
- train teachers in the use of our materials and methods. (Experiencing new activities for themselves is the most effective way for teachers to recognize their value and try them out in their own classes.)
- provide a forum for teachers to come together professionally, share their ideas and resources and discuss issues important to their teaching.

An important and unexpected outcome for the writing team was our own professional development. In order to get our ideas across, we had to learn how to present activities to other teachers, and find within us the confidence to do so. Because we recognized the importance of communicating our ideas we spent time and effort learning how to present activities. A less-experienced person would assist someone with an activity until she was confident to do it herself. This process generated an expanding group of teachers who, through their commitment to improving the maths education of women, were prepared to present their ideas to others.

RESPONSES TO THE MATERIAL

Following the launch of the publication in December 1987 the project is receiving a steady stream of orders from teachers in all states of Australia. The feedback from teachers has been extremely positive and enthusiastic:

> It is very refreshing to find classroom material that uses women's names and non-Anglo names on the presentation of problems and situations. The material values the experience and knowledge of women and helps to break down sex role stereotyping of women and men.
>
> (Vale, 1988)

This encouraging news is coming not only from teachers of adult students but from many secondary teachers:

> An added bonus of this publication is that it is readily transferable to the post-primary class-room and will genuinely provide new beginnings for many students in post-primary schools. While the contexts have been designed to reflect the experiences of adults and particularly

women, many students in post-primary schools will find these contexts familiar to themselves and more appropriate than those presented in mainstream texts.

(Vale, 1988)

FUTURE DIRECTIONS

The loose-leaf format of the resource materials allows for its regular review, revision and updating, as well as the incorporation of additional ideas and lesson plans. There is enormous scope to extend the topics and sessions covered by the materials, and to broaden the accessibility of the sessions by incorporating and adapting methods used for teaching maths to adults of non-English speaking backgrounds.

A further direction for the project is to meet the demand for the distribution of materials to more and more colleagues and other educational bodies in every state of Australia. The provision of in-service training and support to teachers is an integral component of this.

REFERENCES

Dillon, S. (1986) *Jobs for the Girls, Why Not Technical*? Melbourne, Australia: Knowledge Systems Research.

Marr, B. and Helme, S. (eds) (1987) *Mathematics: A New Beginning*. Melbourne: State Training Board.

Vale, C. (1988) Mathematics: a new beginning. *Vinculum* (Journal of the Mathematics Association of Victoria) **25**(1).

Chapter 9

Mathematical Achievement of Grade 12 Girls in Fifteen Countries

Gila Hanna, Erika Kündiger and Christine Larouche

The purpose of this paper is to investigate sex differences in mathematics achievement among students in the last grade of secondary school in a number of North American, European, and East Asian countries. The investigation makes use of the data of the Second International Mathematics Study (SIMS) conducted by the International Association for the Evaluation of Educational Achievement (IEA). The last grade of secondary school, in which the modal student age is about 18, was selected because internationally this represents the population for university entrance. The study used a very large random sample stratified by region and school type in each of the 15 participating countries. Owing to the scale of the study, precise and generalizable conclusions can be drawn about all aspects of the teaching and the learning of mathematics, including the scope of sex differences.

PREVIOUS RESEARCH FINDINGS

In the past two decades, researchers have shown considerable interest in the relationship between the gender and the mathematics achievement of children in the upper grades of elementary school. Many studies to date have shown that by age 13, boys are significantly superior to girls in both their mathematical performance and their attitudes toward mathematics (Backman, 1972; Maccoby and Jacklin, 1974; Mullis, 1975; Aiken, 1976; Benbow and Stanley, 1980) and that the male advantage is especially pronounced among high-scoring exceptionally gifted students, with boys outnumbering girls 13 to 1 (Benbow and Stanley, 1983).

In attempting to explain the male advantage, some research teams have looked at biological differences between the sexes, focusing on hormones (Broverman *et al.*, 1968), genes (Bock and Kolakowski, 1973), and brain organization (Waber, 1979). Other research teams have proposed theoretical models which include a number of factors such as the curriculum, the situation, the environment and participation in mathematics-related science courses (Eccles, 1985; Fennema, 1985; Leder, 1982, 1986). The literature on sex differences has also considered the possibility that male mathematical superiority is due to psychosocial processes such as stereotyped sex-role identifications (Aiken, 1976; Becker, 1981; Burton, 1986; Walden and Walkerdine, 1985) and social reinforcement contingencies (Fox *et al.*, 1979). It should be stressed that some research has also shown that gender-related differences in achievement vary considerably both within and among countries (Schildkamp-Kündiger, 1982). The present investigation was undertaken to pursue the question of regional and international differences in mathematics achievement, particularly in relation to gender.

THE SECOND INTERNATIONAL MATHEMATICS STUDY

The IEA survey sought detailed information from each of the participating countries on three interrelated aspects of mathematics teaching: the intended curriculum, the implemented curriculum and the attained curriculum. A brief description of each follows:

1. The *intended* curriculum is that reflected in curriculum guides, course outlines, syllabuses and textbooks adopted by the educational system. In most countries, nationally defined curricula emanate from a ministry of education or similar national body. In other countries, such as the US, intended goals or specifications of curricular content are often developed by state departments of education or local school districts.
2. The *implemented* curriculum is that actually taught in the classroom. Clearly, the teachers' selection of topics or patterns of emphasis may not be consistent with the intended curriculum. To identify the implemented curriculum, a number of questionnaires were developed for completion by the individual classroom teacher. This highly specific information on curriculum coverage and instructional strategies permits a comprehensive characterization of what mathematics was taught and how it was taught to the target populations.
3. The *attained* curriculum is a measure of what students have learned. Extensive achievement tests were designed to measure students' knowledge and skills in seven areas of mathematics deemed important and appropriate: Sets, Relations and Functions; Number Systems; Algebra; Geometry; Analysis; Probability and Statistics; and Finite Mathematics.

In addition to the investigation of classroom practices, the SIMS study included a survey of student attitudes towards a number of issues related to the study of mathematics. Seven sets of attitude questions addressed the following topics: Mathematics in school; Mathematics as a process; Parental support for Mathematics; Mathematics and myself; Mathematics and society; Mathematics and gender; and Computers and calculators.

The sample

The data derive from the SIMS test administered in 15 different countries to over 40,000 grade 12 students under comparable conditions. The test items, 136 in total, were presented in multiple-choice format (one correct response and four distracters) and divided into seven main content categories: Sets, Relations and Functions (7 items),

Number Systems (19 items), Algebra (25 items), Geometry (28 items), Analysis (46 items), Probability and Statistics (7 items), and Finite Mathematics (4 items).

The student responses were gathered at the end of the course or the school year through a matrix sampling plan, in which each student answered 34 items. As a consequence of using this method, the actual number of respondents to each item was one quarter of the total number of respondents (N) in each country.

For each item, the percentage of correct responses (p-value) was calculated separately for boys and girls in each one of the 15 countries. The mean percentage value for each content category was then obtained by averaging the percentage values for the individual items in that category. Thus the mean and the standard deviation for each content category are based on the item as the unit of analysis (as opposed to the student as the unit of analysis).

To determine whether there were sex differences in achievement the analyses focused on:

1. Overall differences between boys and girls by content category for all countries taken together.
2. Sex differences within and between countries. (Multivariate analyses of variance and paired t-tests were used.)

Analyses and results

The mean percentage values, the standard deviations, and the total number of respondents for the Analysis category (consisting of 46 items) are shown in Table 9.1. Also shown are the number of respondents ranging from a minimum of 747 boys in New Zealand to a maximum of 6174 boys in Japan and from a minimum of 260 girls in Hong Kong to a maximum of 2011 girls in the USA. The achievement levels (mean percentage

Table 9.1. *Descriptive data on the analysis subtest.*

	Girls		Boys	
	N	Mean (sd)	N	Mean (sd)
Belgium Flemish	1155	44 (22)	1677	50 (20)
Belgium French	658	37 (19)	1315	45 (19)
British Columbia	771	20 (17)	1147	22 (17)
Ontario	1110	45 (20)	1744	48 (18)
England	1132	57 (22)	2202	59 (20)
Finland	643	52 (23)	860	59 (21)
Hong Kong	260	66 (15)	844	74 (13)
Hungary	1518	22 (15)	917	32 (17)
Israel	658	43 (23)	888	48 (22)
Japan	1780	60 (15)	6174	71 (13)
New Zealand	424	48 (21)	747	52 (19)
Scotland	643	33 (19)	845	35 (19)
Sweden	658	52 (21)	1867	54 (19)
Thailand	1928	27 (14)	1798	28 (13)
USA	2011	28 (13)	2581	31 (13)
Total (%)	15,349 (37.5)		25,606 (62.5)	

values) show a wide spread for both sexes, ranging from 22 to 74 per cent for boys, and from 20 to 66 per cent for girls.

Differences in achievement by gender

The boxplots in Figure 9.1 display the distribution of the differences in percentage of correct answers for the seven subsets. The major results are as follows:

1. The median difference between girls and boys for the Sets subtest consisting of 7 items was −2. Performance on these 7 items ranged from 42 to 87 per cent with a median of 57 per cent.
2. Performance on the 19 Number Systems items was relatively low, with a mean of 44 per cent and a standard deviation of 21 per cent. The median difference between the

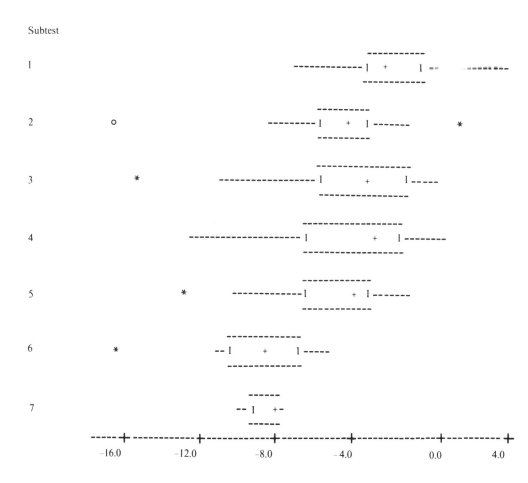

Figure 9.1   *Distribution of differences across seven subtests.*

sexes was −4 per cent. For all but one item the differences were in the boys' favour, ranging from −1 to −7, with a difference of −16 per cent one of the items.

3. On 6 of the 25 items in Algebra there were no differences in correct responses. On the other 19 items the differences ranged from −1 to −15 with a median of −3. The mean performance was 58 per cent with a standard deviation of 18 per cent.

4. Boys did better than girls on all but one of the 28 Geometry items. Differences between the sexes ranged from +1 to −12 with a median of −3. On the whole, achievement on this subtest was low, with only two items exceeding 70 per cent. The mean performance was 38 per cent with a standard deviation of 22 per cent.

5. The Analysis subtest consisted of the largest collection of items (46 items) and yielded a low achievement (mean 45 per cent and standard deviation 15 per cent). The differences ranged from −1 to −12 with a median of −4.

6. On the 7 Probability items the differences ranging from −5 to −16 show that boys performed better than girls on every item. The mean performance was 49 per cent with a standard deviation of 19 per cent.

7. The last subtest consisted of 4 items on which the performance was low (percentage correct were: 54, 43, 49 and 31). The differences were all in the boys' favour: −9, −7, −8 and −8.

Differences by country

Multivariate analysis of variance

Since the same items were administered to all countries, and to two provinces in Canada and in Belgium, the data represent repeated measures of each item, and are certainly not independent or uncorrelated measures, making the assumptions of univariate analysis of variance unrealistic. The advantage of using a multivariate model of analysis of variance is that it allows the country and sex difference results to be intercorrelated or to display different variances without invalidating the *F*-statistic. Hence, the MANOVA model was used to analyse the results of those content categories that contained enough items for such an analysis, namely, Geometry, Analysis, Number Systems, and Algebra. The MANOVA model could not be used for the three content categories, Sets, Probability, and Finite Mathematics, with 7, 7, and 4 items, respectively, because there were too few items.

The results of the four tests of significance of Geometry, Analysis, Number Systems, and Algebra are listed in Table 9.2. It should be noted that since the unit of analysis is the item, the degrees of freedom in the denominator of the *F*-statistic depend on the number of items in the content category being analysed. Thus, the degrees of freedom of the *F*-statistic for the effect of sex on the geometry score would be (1, 27) given that there are 2 sexes and 28 items.

The *F*-statistics for both sex and country are significant. The *F*-statistics for country-by-sex interaction are all significant except for the Number Systems content category. This interaction test is a test of equality of sex differences across countries, and thus its significance indicates that any sex differences that might exist are not consistent across countries.

Table 9.2. *Multivariate analysis of variance: F-values by sex and country for four content categories, population B.*

Source	DF	Geometry (28)	Analysis (46)	Number Systems (19)	Algebra (25)
Sex	1	38.44*	181.40*	33.91*	28.97*
Country	14	16.36*	68.04*	17.29*	10.96*
Country × Sex	14	6.95*	17.07*	1.91	8.82*

*$p < 0.01$

Table 9.3. *Mean percentage differences of correct responses reaching statistical significance at the 0.005 level, by country and content category.*

	Sets (7)	Algebra (25)	Number Systems (19)	Geometry (28)	Finite (4)	Analysis (46)	Probability (7)
Thailand	–	–	–	–	–	–	–
British Columbia	–	–	–	–3	–	–	–
England	–	–	–	–	–	–	–5
Sweden	–	–	–	–	–	–3	–9
New Zealand	–	–	–	–	–12	–4	–12
USA	–	–	–	–3	–5	–3	–9
Ontario	=	–	–4	–2	–10	–4	–12
Scotland	–	–4	–5	–	–3	–2	–9
Hong Kong	–	–3	–5	–5	–4	–9	–
Belgium Flemish	–	–5	–9	–5	–20	–6	–11
Belgium French	–	–9	–5	–6	–13	–9	–9
Finland	–	–6	–6	–7	–15	–7	–18
Israel	–	–6	–5	–5	–12	–5	–15
Japan	–	–3	–5	–5	–3	–10	–5
Hungary	–8	–13	–11	–8	–	–10	–12

Paired t-test analyses

For each country, the mean percentage of correct responses for girls was compared to that for boys, using the paired *t*-test with the item as the unit of analysis. Statistical significance in this context means that if these items were a random sample from a large set of items, then the average difference between the sexes for that set of items would not be zero. (Because there are 15 separate *t*-test analyses, the level of significance was set at 0.005).

The results are presented in Table 9.3. A positive difference in mean percentage correct represents a higher mean percentage for girls and a negative difference a higher mean for boys; a dash (–) indicates that the difference is not statistically significant. Countries in which there were more categories with differences in the girls' favour are at the top of the list (Thailand, British Columbia and England), whereas those in which there were more differences in the boys' favour are at the bottom of the list (Israel, Japan and Hungary). The seven content categories of the test are in order from left (most favourable to girls) to right (least favourable to girls). Thus the first content category is Sets (since this is a subtest in which the boys did better in only one country), followed by Algebra (in which boys did better in eight countries).

As Table 9.3 shows, in Thailand, British Columbia, and England there were almost no differences between girls and boys reaching statistical significance at the 0.005 level. On the other hand, in the last six countries on the list, Belgium Flemish, Belgium French, Finland, Israel, Japan and Hungary, there were several large differences ranging from −3 to −20 percentage points. Looking at each content category separately, it appears that for all but Sets there were significant differences consistently in the boys' favour. The pattern of results indicates that in all but the first three countries on the list, girls were less successful than boys.

In the discussion that follows, we attempt to account for these findings. In particular, we develop the contrast between the first three and the last three countries on the list by examining a series of contextual variables which, potentially, explain these regional differences in mathematics achievement. Some of the most likely explanations, as the reader will see, are *not* supported by the data.

DISCUSSION

Proportion of female maths teachers

Many researchers have suggested that a female's perception of maths as a male domain may negatively affect her motivation to do well in the subject and hence affect her achievement (Fennema and Sherman, 1977; Sherman and Fennema, 1977; Leder, 1982). In fact, it is thought that girls often fear success in mathematics, believing that their social relationships with their male peers will suffer if they are perceived as superior in a sphere that they imagine to be forbidden to women (Moss, 1982). Finn *et al.* (1979) have suggested that girls' performance improves most significantly in programmes that rely on older girls to counsel, encourage, and tutor younger girls.

In this light, it would seem reasonable to suggest that the ratio of female to male maths teachers may be an important factor in explaining sex differences in mathematical achievement, since it most likely affects the degree to which girls subscribe to the notion that maths is the preserve of men. Thus, according to this reasoning, countries with negligible sex differences in achievement would be expected to have higher proportions of female maths teachers than their highly sex-differentiated counterparts. Although this notion seems intuitively sound, as Table 9.4 shows, our data do not support it. For instance, in British Columbia, very small sex differences were observed even though only 3 per cent of the maths teachers were female, while in Hungary very large sex differences emerged despite the fact that a majority of the teachers (60 per cent) were female.

School organization

Another factor that is directly relevant to girls' fear of jeopardizing their relationships with boys as a result of their success in mathematics lies in whether or not boys and girls are segregated in school. Husen (1967) reported that there were fewer sex differences in the interest shown in mathematics in single-sex schools than in mixed schools, most likely because girls in the absence of boys do not experience the sex role conflict.

Again, it would seem reasonable to suggest that fewer sex differences in achievement would be observed among single-sex schools than among mixed ones. Unfortunately,

Table 9.4. *Contextual variables by country: female maths teachers, school organization, years of anticipated post-secondary education and home support.*

	Thailand	British Columbia	England	Israel	Japan	Hungary
Female maths teachers (%)	52	03	30	38	05	60
Students planning 2 or more years of post-secondary education (%)	78	73	93	63	80	92
School organization	mixed	mixed	mixed	mixed	mixed	mixed
Home support Parents encourage maths much or very much (%)	79	77	81	69	44	49
Parents want me to do well much or very much (%)	90	94	95	83	81	80

the six countries with the greatest disparity on test results pertaining to girls' achievement were predominantly mixed so that no test of this hypothesis could be made.

Sex stereotypic thinking

Another way in which one can assess the degree to which students subscribe to traditional ideas about the role of mathematics in men's and women's lives is to ask them questions directly relevant to the problem. This was done in the SIMS by asking boys and girls to respond to four statements and to rate their answers on a scale ranging from strongly agree to strongly disagree. The four statements were as follows: (1) men make better scientists and engineers than women; (2) boys have more natural ability in mathematics than girls; (3) boys need to know more mathematics than girls; and (4) a woman needs a career just as much as a man does.

Another reasonable hypothesis about sex differences in achievement would then be that girls in countries with few sex differences would be less inclined to subscribe to the notion that maths is the preserve of men than girls in those countries where large sex differences are found (Israel, Japan, and Hungary, in the case of this study). However, as Figure 9.2 illustrates, this hypothesis is not supported by our data. Interestingly, however, in all six countries, girls were significantly less likely than boys to perceive maths as a male domain (the higher the bar, the less stereotypic the answer). Thus, it does not appear that achievement in mathematics is directly related to the perception of mathematics as described in the four statements mentioned above.

Years of anticipated post-secondary education

Another factor that may affect sex differences in mathematical achievement is the degree to which boys and girls in a given country plan on pursuing further education. In

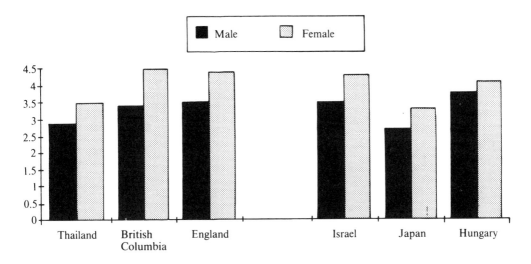

Figure 9.2 *Sex stereotyping by country. (The higher the bar the more support is given to the perception of equality of males and females in mathematics.)*

effect, it has been suggested that expectations and beliefs of the learner and of the wider society have a bearing on achievement (Leder, 1986). Perhaps girls' relatively lower achievement is partly due to their lower level of educational aspiration in the countries where important sex differences in mathematics achievement are in fact observed.

Again, this hypothesis is not supported by our data. Girls in the countries with large sex differences were no more likely to have inferior educational aspirations relative to their male peers than girls in countries with no sex differences (see Table 9.4).

Home support

Since mathematics is often perceived as a male domain, it is probable that in certain environments parents give more support to mathematical learning for boys than for girls. In fact, Fennema and Sherman (1977) have reported that girls report less home support for their mathematical endeavours.

Again, it would be conceivable that such differential support could affect the achievement of females. Perhaps, in countries where large sex differences are observed, parents give more support to their male offspring than to their female offspring while such differential treatment may be less evident in countries where no differences are observed between the sexes. However, no evidence of this is present in our data (See Table 9.5).

Another way in which home support may be responsible for sex differences in

Table 9.5. *Home support by country by sex.*

		Thailand	British Columbia	England	Israel	Japan	Hungary
Parents encourage maths (much or very much) (%)	Boys	77	79	80	70	45	62
	Girls	82	76	81	68	45	52
Parents want me to do well (much or very much) (%)	Boys	89	96	96	87	81	87
	Girls	91	94	93	76	79	75

mathematical achievement lies in the degree to which support is provided for mathematical tasks. Since boys are traditionally reinforced for their participation in masculine activities by society at large, perhaps the degree of home support is more important for girls than for boys in predicting achievement. Accordingly, sex differences should be less pronounced in countries whose mean level of parental support is relatively high than in countries in which home support is less evident.

Our data support this idea. The countries where sex differences were negligible showed high levels of home support for both sexes, whereas the countries where important sex differences were observed showed lower levels of home support (see Table 9.5). Furthermore, in two countries, Israel and Hungary, girls reported receiving less support than boys did for mathematical achievement.

CONCLUSIONS

The SIMS examination of a number of contextual variables was an attempt at identifying situations that might be related to significant sex differences in mathematics achievement. The analyses indicated that differences in achievement could not be attributed to these variables. This does not mean that these variables have no influence on mathematical learning, but rather that their influence may be exerted in interaction with other societal factors. The study highlights the fact that the issue of gender differences in mathematics is very complex and should be explored from many different perspectives.

The analysis of the achievement results shows that gender differences in mathematics vary from country to country. Since it is very unlikely that biological differences between the sexes vary from one country to another, the SIMS data tend to contradict those theories that attempt to explain boys' superiority in mathematics on the basis of biological factors.

REFERENCES

Aiken, L.R. (1976) Update on attitudes and other affective variables in learning mathematics. *Review of Educational Research*, **46**, 293–311.

Backman, M.E. (1972) Patterns of mental abilities: ethnic, socioeconomic, and sex differences. *American Educational Research Journal*, **9**, 1–12.

Becker, J.R. (1981) Differential treatment of females and males in mathematics classes. *Journal for Research in Mathematics Education*, **12**(1), 40–53.

Benbow, C.P. and Stanley, J.C. (1980) Sex differences in mathematical ability: fact or artifact? *Science*, **210**, 1262–1264.

Benbow, C.P. and Stanley, J.C. (1983) Sex differences in mathematical reasoning ability: more facts. *Science*, **222**, 1029–1031.

Bock, D.R. and Kolakowski, D. (1973) Further evidence of major-gene influence on human spatial visualizing ability. *American Journal of Human Genetics*, **25**, 1–14.

Broverman, D.M., Klaiber, E.L., Kobayashi, Y. and Vogel, W. (1968) Roles of activation and inhibition in sex differences in cognitive abilities. *Psychological Review*, **75**, 23–50.

Burton, L. (ed.) (1986) *Girls into Maths Can Go*. London: Holt, Rinehart and Winston.

Eccles, J. (1985) Model of students' mathematics enrolment decisions. *Educational Studies in Mathematics*, **16**, 303–320.

Fennema, E. (ed.) (1985) Explaining sex-related differences in mathematics: theoretical models. *Educational Studies in Mathematics*, **16**(3), 303–320.

Fennema, E. and Sherman, J.A. (1977) Sex-related differences in mathematics achievement, spatial visualization, and affective factors. *American Educational Research Journal*, **14**, 51–71.

Finn, J.D., Dulberg, L. and Reis, J. (1979) Sex differences in educational attainment: a cross-national perspective. *Harvard Educational Review*, **49**, 477–503.

Fox L.H., Tobin, D. and Brody, L. (1979) Sex-role socialization and achievement in mathematics. In Wittig, M.A. and Peterson, A.C. (eds) *Sex-related Differences in Cognitive Functioning*. New York: Academic Press.

Husen, T. (ed.) (1967) *International Study of Achievement in Mathematics: A Comparison of Twelve Countries*, Vols I and II. New York: John Wiley.

Leder, G.C. (1982) Mathematics achievement and fear of success. *Journal for Research in Mathematics Education*, **13**(2), 124–125.

Leder, G.C. (1986) *Gender Linked Differences in Mathematics Learning: Further Explorations*. Paper presented at the Research Presession to the NCTM 64th Annual meeting, Washington, DC, April 1986.

Maccoby, E. and Jacklin, C. (1974) *The Psychology of Sex Differences*. Stanford, CA: Stanford University Press.

Moss, J.D. (1982) *Towards Equality: Progress by Girls in Mathematics in Australian Secondary Schools*. The Australian Council for Educational Research Limited, Radford House, Frederick Street, Hawthorn 3122, Victoria, Australia.

Mullis, I.V.S. (1975) *Educational Achievement and Sex Discrimination*. Denver, CO: National Assessment of Educational Progress.

Schildkamp-Kündiger, E. (ed.) (1982) *International Review on Gender and Mathematics*. Columbus, OH: ERIC Clearinghouse for Science, Mathematics and Environmental Education.

Sherman, J.A. and Fennema, E. (1977) The study of mathematics by high school girls and boys: variables. *American Educational Research Journal*, **14**, 159–168.

Waber, D.P. (1979) Cognitive abilities and sex-related variations in the maturation of cerebral cortical functions. In Wittig, M.A. and Petersen, A.C. (eds) *Sex-related Differences in Cognitive Functioning*. New York: Academic Press.

Walden, R. and Walkerdine, V. (1985) *Girls and Mathematics: From Primary to Secondary Schooling*. London: Institute of Education, University of London.

Chapter 10

Girls and Mathematics in Singapore: The Case of GCE 'O' Level Mathematics

Berinderjeet Kaur

Mathematics plays an important role in our daily lives and a thorough grounding in it is essential for all boys and girls during their education and training. Although mathematics is a compulsory (core) subject to age 16 in Singapore schools, it does not follow that all pupils actively participate, or that their potentiality to succeed is necessarily equal.

In a study carried out by the writer which compared the performance of Singapore boys and girls in the UK based Ordinary Level mathematics (syllabus D) it was found that, on the whole, the girls were out-performed by the boys.

THE STUDY

Design

Sample

Out of a population of 42,627 Singapore candidates (21,037 boys and 21,590 girls) who took the November/December 1986 GCE 'O' level mathematics examination, a random sample of 176 (88 boys and 88 girls) was used for the study. The breakdown of the sample by ability grades is shown in Table 10.1.

Table 10.1. *Sample of 'O' level mathematics students studied.*

Grade	No. of girls	No. of boys	Total
A	15	15	30
B	14	14	28
C	13	13	26
D	17	17	34
E	15	15	30
U	14	14	28
Total	88	88	176

Principal objectives of the study

Taking the GCE 'O' level examination results in mathematics as a standard of mathematics attainment, the principal objectives of the study were as follows:

1. To locate sex differences in mathematics attainment and to note any pattern of such differences, using the following methods:
   (a) Compare the total marks on:
      (i) Paper I
      (ii) Paper II
      (iii) Paper II Section A
      (iv) Paper II Section B
   (b) Compare marks for all parts of the questions in both papers.
   (c) Identify parts of the questions in both papers on which the difference in performance was statistically significant.
   (d) Compare preference for questions, given choice (applicable only to Section B of Paper II).
   (e) Compare performance on compulsory questions grouped by topics.
   (f) Compare performance on compulsory questions which test spatial ability.
2. To compare pupils' performance in Mathematics in relation to the other subjects they took in the examination and identify any sex differences which may exist.

Design in relation to statistical and computing aspects

The main technical function of any research design is to control variance. The statistical principle behind this mechanism is: maximize systematic variance, control extraneous systematic variance and minimize error variance (Kerlinger, 1964, p. 280). For the purpose of the present study, it was easy to satisfy the first condition, since there were only two groups (boys and girls) under consideration. For the control of extraneous variables, there are three main methods to minimize their effects. First, one can choose subjects so that they are as homogeneous as possible; secondly, whenever possible, randomly assign subjects to the experimental groups and conditions and randomly assign conditions and other factors to experimental groups; thirdly, an extraneous variable can be built into the research design as an assigned variable, thus achieving control and yielding additional research information (Kerlinger, 1964, p. 284). In the present study there were many extraneous variables to be considered, for example, intelligence, motivation, attitude, social class, teaching methods, type of school and last but not least the subject options of each candidate. The present study has adopted the first method, as in both groups (boys and girls) there were equal numbers of the same ability (i.e. grade).

The error variance is associated with individual differences among subjects. Owing to random selection of sample data it was expected that the variance will be minimized. However, another source of error variance is that associated with error of measurement. The examination board authorities are usually very careful with their examination marking and indeed a good number of sample scripts were double marked.

The data

The 'O' level results were recorded with letter grades A, B, C, D, E, U; A representing the top and U the bottom of the ability range. The examination consisted of two papers, each of two and a half hours duration, based on the University of Cambridge Local Examinations Syndicate's 'O' Level Mathematics syllabus D. Paper I has 28 compulsory short questions; the first 20 each carry 3 marks while the next 8 each carry 5 marks. Paper II Section A has 5 compulsory questions which carry 52 marks while Section B has 7 questions of which the candidate is to answer 4 and each carries 12 marks. Marks gained for every part of a question on both papers were recorded and used for data analysis.

Statistical aspects

There are several ways to analyse the same data and no method of analysis is perfect. After the collection of data, the first task was to obtain descriptive statistics. For all the parts of the questions in both papers the means and standard deviations (s.d.) for the two groups were tabulated. For Paper II Section B questions the frequency distribution table was constructed. Vertical and horizontal bar charts were used where appropriate to display the data collected.

The main purpose of the data analysis was to find sex differences in mathematics attainment. These are best tested by using the statistical method of the analysis of variance—the total variance is broken down into two major component sources of variance, between-groups variance and within-groups variance. The one-way analysis of variance test was considered unsuitable for the present study as the two groups under consideration had their subjects matched by ability and for both groups the sample was constructed to represent all grade levels in approximately equal proportions which resulted in the sample being fairly uniformly distributed over the entire ability range.

The two-way analysis of variance test was used extensively in the present study as it was able to control the other known sources of variances, particularly ability levels, which was not possible with the one-way analysis of variance test.

Computing aspects

Computer programs for statistical data analysis, contained in the Programmed Methods for Multivariate Data (PMMD) package (Youngman, 1975, 1976) were used. This package contains a set of programs designed to serve the analysis needs of both research workers and students in the social sciences. For the present study only simple and most appropriate statistical methods were used to analyse the data.

The CATT and CATM programs were used to obtain the means and standard deviations to all parts of the questions in both papers. The AVAR program was used to carry out the two-way analysis of variance giving significance-level marking and probability values for the test of various effects. The CATM program was also used to calculate the

Pearson product-moment correlation coefficient for the sample's performance in mathematics and other subjects taken in the examination.

Analysis of the examination papers

The questions were classified by topic and test of spatial ability. Using the elementary mathematics syllabus for the New Education System, Singapore, as a guideline the questions were categorized under the specific topics—Arithmetic; Mensuration; Algebra and Graphs; Geometry; Trigonometry; Statistics; Sets; Probability; Vectors in Two Dimensions; and Matrices and Transformations. As long as a question contained a spatial element it was categorized under test of spatial ability, although some pupils who have encountered similar problems before may use only rote-learned skills. Tables 10.2 and 10.3 show the classification of the questions by topic and test of spatial ability respectively.

Table 10.2. *Questions grouped by topic.*

Topic	Paper I	Paper II
Arithmetic	1ai, 1aii, 1b, 2a, 2bi, 2bii, 4a, 4b, 4c, 9a, 9b, 14i, 14ii, 19i, 19ii, 19iii, 20a, 27i	1ai, 1aii, 1bi, 1bii, 8i, 8ii, 8iii, 8iv, 8v
Mensuration	24i, 24ii, 24iii, 27ii, 28ii, 28iii	6ia, 6ib, 6ii, 6iii
Algebra and Graphs	6a, 6b, 6c, 11, 12a, 12b, 15i, 15ii, 20b, 22ai, 22aii, 22b	2ai, 2aii, 2aiii, 2b, 2c, 9i, 9ii, 9iii, 9iv, 9v, 9vi
Geometry	5i, 5ii, 5iii, 16i, 16ii, 16iii, 27iii	5ai, 5aii, 5aiii, 5bi, 5bii, 5biii, 5biv
Trigonometry	7i, 7ii, 13i, 13ii, 26i, 26ii, 28i	3a, 3b, 3c, 7a, 7bi, 7bii, 7biii, 7biv, 10i, 10ii, 10iii, 10iv
Statistics	18i, 18ii, 21i, 21ii, 21iii	12i, 12ii, 12iii, 12iv, 12v, 12vi
Sets	3a, 3bi, 3bii, 8i, 8ii, 8iii	
Probability	25i, 25ii, 25iiia, 25iiib	
Vectors in two dimensions	17i, 17ii, 17iii	11ia, 11ib, 11ic, 11ii, 11iii, 11iv, 11v, 11vi
Matrices and Transformations	10i, 10ii, 23i, 23ii, 23iii	4i, 4ii, 4iii, 4iv

Table 10.3. *Compulsory questions which test spatial ability.*

Paper I	Paper II
5i, 5ii, 5iii, 7i, 7ii, 10i, 10ii, 13i, 13ii, 15i, 15ii, 16i, 16ii, 16iii, 17i, 17ii, 17iii, 21i, 21ii, 21iii, 23i, 23ii, 23iii, 24i, 24ii, 24iii, 26i, 26ii, 27ii, 27iii, 28i, 28ii, 28iii	3a, 3b, 3c, 4i, 4ii, 4iii, 4iv, 5ai, 5aii, 5aiii, 5bi, 5bii, 5biii, 5biv

The marks gained for every part of a question on both papers were recorded and used to:

(a) Compute the total marks on:
    (i) Paper I
    (ii) Paper II
    (iii) Paper II Section A
    (iv) Paper II Section B
    (v) Compulsory questions for each of the ten topics
    (vi) Compulsory questions which test spatial ability
    for every pupil and locate any differences in attainment by the two sexes
(b) Compute the means and standard deviations of marks for all parts of the questions in both papers for the two groups (boys and girls) and locate any differences in attainment.
(c) Construct the frequency table for questions in Paper II Section B.

Statement of results

The population

Before reporting the results of the present study, some general facts and figures are given in Table 10.4 regarding Singapore's population (all the candidates, who took the 'O' level, syllabus D November/December 1986 examination).

Since C is a pass grade, it is reasonable to divide the pass grades into two categories—grades A and B as an upper-grade pass and C as a lower-grade pass. The third category is the fail grade—grades, D, E and U. From Table 10.4 the following further observations can be noted:

	Male (%)		Female (%)		Overall (%)	
Upper-grade pass (A, B)	64.1	⎤	56.0	⎤	60.0	⎤
		78.4		72.0		75.2
Lower-grade pass (C)	14.3	⎦	16.0	⎦	15.2	⎦
Fail grade (D, E, U)	21.6		28.0		24.8	

Seventy-five per cent of the candidates passed the examination. A higher proportion of the boys obtained an upper-grade pass while a higher proportion of the girls obtained a lower-grade pass and the fail grade. A sex by grade (2 × 6) chi-square test was performed

Table 10.4. *Singapore's population results—grade by sex.*

Grade	No. of males (%)	No. of females (%)	Total (%)
A	8114 (38.6)	6620 (30.7)	14734 (34.6)
B	5364 (25.5)	5473 (25.3)	10837 (25.4)
C	3012 (14.3)	3452 (16.0)	6464 (15.2)
D	1009 (4.8)	1361 (6.3)	2370 (5.5)
E	835 (4.0)	1108 (5.1)	1943 (4.6)
U	2703 (12.8)	3576 (16.6)	6279 (14.7)
Total	21037 (100)	21590 (100)	42627 (100)

Table 10.5. *Chi-square test for sex by grade results.*

Sex	Grade					
	A	B	C	D	E	U
M	8114	5364	3012	1009	835	2703
(21037)						
F	6620	5473	3452	1361	1108	3576
(21590)						
42627	14734	10837	6464	2370	1943	6279

		A	B	C	D	E	U
$\dfrac{fo^2}{frfc}$	M	0.2124	0.1262	0.0667	0.0204	0.0171	0.0553
	F	0.1378	0.1280	0.0854	0.0362	0.0293	0.0943
Total		0.3502	0.2542	0.1521	0.0566	0.0464	0.1496

$$\sum \frac{fo^2}{frfc} = 1.0091$$

Degrees of freedom $= (2 - 1)(6 - 1) = 5$

$X^2 = 42627\,(1.0091 - 1)$
    $= 387.9057$
from tables $p < 0.001$ (highly significant)

on the data in Table 10.4 and the result was statistically highly significant ($p < 0.01$), which shows that the results of the boys were significantly better than those of the girls in 'O' level mathematics (Table 10.5).

Analysis of total marks on the papers

Table 10.6 summarizes the results of the two-way analysis of variance for Sex by Ability for the total marks on Paper I (Variable 1), and Paper II (Variable 2), Paper II Section A (Variable 3) and Paper II Section B (Variable 4). For all four variables the analysis showed highly significant markings for the condition Ability. Only variable 1 has a highly significant marking for the condition Sex. This means that the difference in performance on Paper I was highly significant for the two sexes and the boys did significantly better (mean 54.06; s.d. 23.27) than the girls (mean 50.87, s.d. 24.07).

For variable 2 (Paper II) a significant marking for Sex/Ability interaction was present. This was due to the mean scores of the boys for Ability grades A, B, C and U being higher than the girls but not so for grades D and E. There were slightly significant markings for Sex/Ability interaction for variables 3 and 4.

Preference for questions in Paper II Section B

Table 10.7 summarizes the questions attempted by the boys and girls by ability groups in Paper II Section B. From Figure 10.1 it may be seen that girls showed a marked preference for question 9 (Algebra and Graphs) and question 11 (Vectors in two dimensions) with the test of difference of proportions showing a highly significant

Table 10.6. *Two-way analysis of variance for sex by ability.*

		Source	m.s.	d.f.	F-ratio	Probability
Variable 1: Paper I		Total	563.619	175		
		Between	8369.482	11		
Sex	mean (s.d.)	Sex	445.830	1	11.1304	0.0014**
		Ability	18306.768	5	457.0376	0.0000**
Female	50.87 (24.07)	Sex by Ability	16.926	5	0.4226	0.8337
Male	54.06 (23.27)	Within	40.055	164		
Variable 2: Paper II		Total	567.957	175		
		Between	8458.332	11		
Sex	mean (s.d.)	Sex	28.406	1	0.7335	0.6026
		Ability	18508.649	5	477.9579	0.0000**
Female	46.50 (23.54)	Sex by Ability	94.000	5	2.4274	0.0369*
Male	47.30 (24.11)	Within	38.724	164		
Variable 3: Paper II Section A		Total	124.903	175		
		Between	1626.424	11		
Sex	mean (s.d.)	Sex	4.436	1	0.1834	0.6729
		Ability	3522.765	5	145.6243	0.0000**
Female	26.51 (11.55)	Sex by Ability	54.479	5	2.2521	0.0509?
Male	26.83 (10.73)	Within	24.191	164		
Variable 4: Paper II Section B		Total	185.830	175		
		Between	2711.789	11		
Sex	mean (s.d.)	Sex	10.390	1	0.6333	0.5669
		Ability	5928.618	5	361.3620	0.0000**
Female	19.99 (12.92)	Sex by Ability	35.239	5	2.1479	0.0616?
Male	20.48 (14.34)	Within	16.406	164		

? slightly significant $p < 0.1$; * significant $p < 0.05$; ** highly significant $p < 0.01$.
s.d., standard deviation; m.s., mean sum of squares; d.f., degrees of freedom.

Table 10.7. *Frequency table of questions attempted in Paper II Section B by sex and overall ability in mathematics.*

Question Number	Sex	Ability						Total
		A	B	C	D	E	U	
6	F	9	9	8	7	8	4	45
	M	13	7	10	11	6	7	54
7	F	12	11	12	15	10	6	66
	M	12	10	9	14	11	8	64
8	F	10	8	5	6	7	3	39
	M	11	9	6	5	6	0	37
9	F	10	10	9	7	13	3	52
	M	3	4	8	8	5	3	31
10	F	7	8	3	4	2	4	28
	M	11	10	4	3	2	5	35
11	F	9	7	8	14	9	10	57
	M	7	9	8	10	7	2	43
12	F	3	3	6	11	8	8	39
	M	3	6	5	10	10	6	40

F, female; M, male.

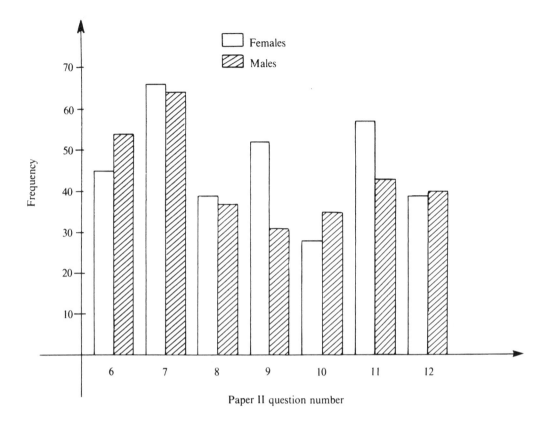

Figure 10.1 *Pupils' preferences for questions in Paper II Section B.*

difference ($p < 0.01$) for question 9 and a significant difference ($p < 0.05$) for question 11. Boys showed a preference for question 6 (Mensuration) and question 10 (Trigonometry—latitude and longitude) but the test of difference of proportions only showed a slightly significant ($p < 0.1$) difference for question 6.

Analysis of questions grouped by topics

The analysis showed highly significant levels for the condition Ability across all 10 variables (topics). Only variables 6 (Mensuration) and 10 (Statistics) have highly significant markings for the condition Sex. For both Mensuration and Statistics the boys performed better than the girls. Variables 5 (Arithmetic), 7 (Algebra and Graphs) and 8 (Geometry) have significant markings for the condition Sex. The boys performed better than the girls on Arithmetic and Geometry but not on Algebra and Graphs. On variable 5 (Arithmetic) a significant marking for Sex/Ability interaction was present. This was due to the mean scores of the girls for Ability grades A, B, D, E and U being lower than the boys but not so for grade C. Variable 12 (Probability) has a slightly significant marking for the condition Sex and the boys performed better than the girls.

Analysis of questions which test spatial ability

It may be seen from Table 10.8 that for both conditions, Ability and Sex, the markings were highly significant. The boys (mean 39.32; s.d. 19.51) were superior to the girls (mean 36.60; s.d. 20.74) in performance on questions that contained a spatial element.

Pupils' performance in mathematics in relation to the other subjects they took in the English medium examination

Altogether there were 20 subjects, which were taken by the sample collectively, although each pupil only took eight or less. The Pearson's product-moment correlation co-efficients (where possible) were calculated using the PMMD. CATM programme for the boys, girls and total sample. Table 10.9 summarizes the correlation coefficients

It may be seen that Additional Mathematics correlated highly significantly and also closely with Mathematics for both sexes; and this is not surprising as only a pupil who is very good in Mathematics in secondary two in Singapore is allowed to do it. Not all mathematics-related subjects (Physics, Science (Chemistry, Physics) and Metalwork) correlated to the same degree for the two sexes; this may be due to a number of under-lying causes, some of which may be attributed to teaching styles, concentration on certain aspects of the curriculum only and ratio of boys to girls in a class taking the particular subject.

DISCUSSION

The analysis of the GCE 'O' level mathematics results of the population of this present study reveals that on the whole boys do perform better than girls. This is a similar finding to other studies (DES, 1980; Sharma and Meighan, 1980), which compare the performance of boys and girls in mathematics attainment. The contribution of this present study is to suggest areas of concern in mathematics attainment where boys and girls differ significantly in performance when matched by ability.

Table 10.8. *Two-way analysis of variance for Sex by Ability.*

		Source	m.s.	d.f.	F-ratio	Probability
Variable 18		Total	407.963	175		
Spatial ability		Between	5813.164	11		
		Sex	324.867	1	7.1527	0.0082**
Sex	Mean (s.d.)	Ability	12692.533	5	279.4550	0.0000**
		Sex by Ability	31.454	5	0.6925	0.6323
Female	36.60 (20.74)	Within	45.419	164		
Male	39.32 (19.51)					

**highly significant $p < 0.01$.

Table 10.9. *Correlation coefficients (frequency values in brackets) between performance in Mathematics and other subjects in the English medium.*

Subject	Boys	Girls	Total sample
Additional maths	0.8547 ** (20)	0.8094 ** (20)	0.8338 ** (40)
Physics	0.8923 ** (12)	0.3550 (10)	0.8157 ** (22)
Chemistry	0.9129 * (5)	0.8783 (4)	0.7693 * (9)
Combined science	1.0000 ** (3)	0.3705 (7)	0.5151 (10)
Science (Chemistry, Physics)	0.5215 ** (44)	0.7385 ** (32)	0.5745 ** (76)
Science (Chemistry, Biology)	0.7419 * (8)	0.8508 ** (11)	0.7923 ** (19)
Biology	– 0.5000 (3)	0.9623 * (4)	0.3536 (7)
Human and Social Biology	0.6446 * (10)	0.5750 * (18)	0.5854 ** (28)
English language	0.4766 ** (87)	0.4989 ** (88)	0.4877 ** (175)
English literature	0.4140 ** (41)	– 0.0950 (44)	0.1504 (85)
Geography	0.9007 ** (21)	0.4866 ** (28)	0.6182 ** (49)
History	0.4481 * (21)	0.1604 (18)	0.3103? (39)
Art	0.2439 (43)	0.0840 (42)	0.1760 (85)
Food and Nutrition	No data (0)	0.8677 * (7)	0.8677 * (7)
Fashion and Fabric	No data (0)	0.0000 (2)	0.0000 (2)
Bible knowledge	0.1838 (18)	0.5739 ** (19)	0.3955 * (37)
Commerce	insufficient (1) data	insufficient (1) data	– 1.0000 ** (2)
Principle of Accounts	insufficient (1) data	0.4824 (7)	0.6396? (8)
Metalwork	0.6308 ** (24)	0.5556 (4)	0.5890 ** (28)

** highly significant ($p < 0.01$); * significant ($p < 0.05$); ? slightly significant ($p < 0.1$).

This present study has examined the performance in mathematics of a sample (which was so constructed to have equal numbers of boys and girls of the same ability grade across the ability range) of Singapore candidates in the GCE 'O' level examination and found significant differences between the performance of boys and girls in the following areas. Boys performed better than the girls on Paper I questions on the whole and in particular on questions 2a, 9b, 24iii, 27iii and 28ii. For the compulsory questions on both papers boys did significantly better than the girls on the following topics—Mensuration, Statistics, Arithmetic, Geometry and Probability while the girls out-performed the boys on Algebra and Graphs. Boys also surpassed the girls on the compulsory questions that tested spatial ability. In Paper II Section B girls showed a marked preference for questions on Algebra and Graphs, and Vectors in two-dimensions, while the boys' only marked preference was the question on Mensuration. Ability grades in Physics, Science (Chemistry, Physics) and Metalwork 'O' level examinations did not correlate with Mathematics grades to the same degree for the two sexes.

POSSIBLE REASONS FOR OBSERVED DIFFERENCES

It is interesting to note that the few questions in Paper I on which girls surpassed boys were generally of the type that call for recognition or classification, application of techniques, substitution of numbers into an algebraic expression and so forth, just the kinds of operations that are most susceptible to drilling. These questions mainly centred on the topics Arithmetic, Sets, Algebra and Graphs, Vectors in two-dimensions, Trigonometry, and Matrices and Transformations. The fact that these questions were from any particular topic or groups of topics may be irrelevant; as Benford (1976) points out, children 'learn' vectors in much the same way as they learn long division. It appears that rote-learning is more congenial to females (Wood, 1977), and Jones (1973) in his study notes that there appears to be a female tendency to keep to methods they have been taught, to reproduce techniques, to show caution, to avoid being wrong and generally to use a method with which they feel most confident and secure and which is approved by the teacher. This may, perhaps, be due to girls' supposed greater conformity and passive-dependency as opposed to boys' supposed greater independence and activity, differences which, however, may be entirely a product of the social learning involved in the acquisition of sex-roles (Maccoby and Jacklin, 1974).

There were altogether five parts of questions in Paper I on which the boys surpassed the girls highly significantly, one of which was as follows:

9(b) An amount of $80 is shared among three people in the ratio 1 : 6 : 9. Find the difference between the largest and smallest shares.

This problem—which in essence is about proportionality—exposed girls' weakness in this area, which may in turn help to explain their inferior performance on the probability question (number 25). Incidentally, the American NAEP (1975) found that from age 13 onwards boys out-performed girls in the area of probability and statistics. It is interesting that Jones (1973) studying 11-year-olds should have noticed that girls have greater difficulty comparing the magnitude of two fractions and should have speculated whether this leads to a greater difficulty with proportion later on in their learning. Cable (1976) attributes this weakness of being unable to cope with problems on proportionality to 'comparison factors'. Fractions and proportions are examples of comparison factors and what Cable is saying is that one cannot get anywhere with quantification or measurement unless one feels comfortable with comparison factors. Are girls then not comfortable with comparison factors? Would certain teaching styles and methods put girls at ease with comparison factors?

Girls' weakness at spatial visualization has already been mentioned. Questions 24(iii), 27(iii) and 28(ii) all contained a spatial element. Analysis of results showed that boys out-performed the girls markedly on all of them. For question 24(iii), shown in Figure 10.2, the inability to visualize a rearrangement of the figure may have led the girls into complex calculations eventually resulting in an incorrect response.

Question 27(iii) was as follows:

Use as much of the information below as is necessary to answer the following questions. The areas of two similar figures are in the ratio 9 : 50. Given that the length of one side of the smaller figure is 30 cm, find the length of the corresponding side of the larger figure.

$$[\sqrt{5} = 2.24, \sqrt{50} = 7.07]$$

This question involved a comparison factor coupled with spatial visualization of a figure (left to the imagination of the pupil) in two dimensions. Question 28(ii) (see Fig. 10.3) involved the calculation of the volume of a three-dimensional solid block drawn on a two-dimensional piece of paper and called for some form of spatial visualization too.

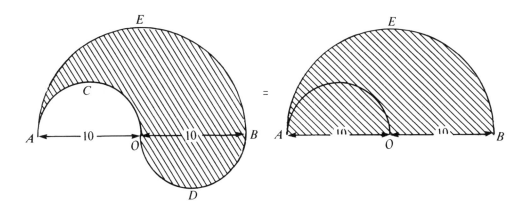

Figure 10.2

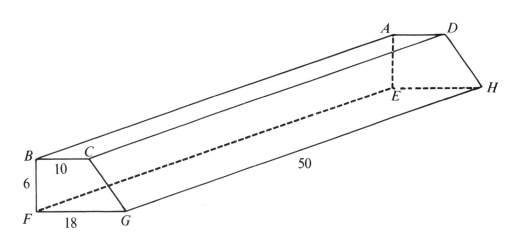

Figure 10.3   Question 28(ii): The diagram represents a solid block of wood of length 50 cm. The faces *ABCD* and *EFGH* are horizontal rectangles. The faces *ABFE, BCGF* and *ADHE* are vertical. *BC* = *AD* = 10 cm, *BF* = *AE* = 6 cm and *FG* = *EH* = 18 cm. Calculate the volume of the book.

Table 10.10. *Number of pupils with technical-related experience who had a correct response to the stated question.*

	Question number		
Sex	24iii	27iii	28ii
Boys (n = 24)	9	3	14
Girls (n = 4)	2	0	2

It may be said that the study of a technical subject like metalwork helps pupils in these three questions (24iii, 27iii, 28ii) and since more boys than girls study this subject it is not surprising that there is a significant difference in performance between the two sexes on such problems. However, in the present study, this was not found to be the case as may be seen from Table 10.10, which summarizes the correct responses to the three questions of the 24 boys and 4 girls in the sample who had technical subject (metalwork) related experience. It is likely then that such observed differences may have their roots elsewhere.

It appears then that girls are most vulnerable on two classes of problem, those involving what Cable (1976) calls quantification and those involving spatial visualization. There has been a tendency to treat the last class as quite separate and distinct, but perhaps the two are related. The struggles girls have with the understanding of ideas like fractions—and, as Cable (1976) notes, it is now being realized that fractions are much more difficult conceptually than was formerly imagined—may be just another expression of their deficit in spatial ability, reflecting a greater capacity on the part of boys to perceive, recognize and assimilate patterns within the conceptual structure of mathematics. If spatial awareness is genetically controlled and sex-linked, girls may get off on the wrong foot with the mathematics that matters before they start learning in earnest.

It may be speculated from the preference of questions where there was a choice and also the topics on which one sex performed markedly better than the other, that Algebra and Graphs was the topic for the girls and Mensuration the topic for the boys. At the ordinary level, Algebra and Graphs centres mainly on computational skills (substitution of numbers into an algebraic expression) and application of techniques such as factorization, drawing a graph, etc. on which girls appeared to be better in this present study. Although both questions (numbers 9 and 11) for which the girls showed a marked preference in Paper II Section B had diagrams to aid the question it may not be true that girls are attracted to such questions, as question 6 (Mensuration) for which the boys showed a marked preference also had a diagram. Boys have been reported to be significantly better than girls on measures (DES, 1980). In the present study this perhaps holds the cue to boys' marked preference for the question on Mensuration.

It is interesting to note from Table 10.9 that the correlation coefficients between the performance of Mathematics and Physics for the boys and girls were significantly different. Physics is often spoken of as a mathematics-related subject, yet the girls' scores in Mathematics and Physics seem to be weakly correlated. It may well be because

Physics is a 'male-orientated' subject which puts the girls off, but as Mathematics is compulsory for all Singapore pupils in the secondary school and a decisive factor for further/higher education opportunities, girls have had no choice but to make the best of the situation. Boys' Mathematics scores correlated negatively (-0.5000) with Biology, while that of girls' correlated highly (0.9623). This means that achievement in Biology was directly and closely related to that in Mathematics for girls but definitely not for boys.

Fennema and Sherman (1977) reported that sex differences in performance were linked to sex-related differences in attitude. In a society like Singapore's, which differentiates role in terms of gender, it follows that individual behaviour will be influenced by what is considered to be sexually appropriate. Since the expenditure of time and energy on any task is contingent upon the value that has been assigned to it, tasks that are considered to be not useful or sexually inappropriate will be ignored in favour of more appropriate or useful tasks. If society deems that engineers and scientists are men, then physics, mathematics and mechanical activities are the province of males, and if nurses, secretaries and social scientists are women, then biology, literature and social studies are the province of females; these judgements will be reflected in the amount of effort expended by girls and boys on these subjects.

The present study has shown that among Singapore pupils the boys achieved better results than the girls at Mathematics. Driver (1980) explains the superior performance of West Indian girls on mathematics as compared to West Indian boys in terms of the aspirations and achievements of young West Indian pupils in whose culture the women, rather than their husbands or brothers, are the guardians of their family's good name and the providers of its staple income. In Asian (Singapore) society men are traditionally the family providers. Is it then surprising that the aspirations of the boys in Singapore are reflected in their performance in Mathematics?

CONCLUSION

To say that the present study has compared boys and girls of the type like with like by merely matching them in ability—defined by the score on an examination—is not true, as mathematics-related experiences in other subjects, the variation between schools and within schools which may be present due to different specializations and type of school (single-sex or co-educational) besides other variables, some of which may be motivation, intelligence, social class, teacher attitude and teaching methods, have not been considered. Although the examination scores have been used to pass judgement on spatial ability, one must not rule out the possibility of pupils being drilled on examination type questions. In most, if not all, secondary graduating classes in Singapore the past year's mathematics examination papers of the Syndicate are an integral part of the classroom written exercises in an attempt to 'master' examination-type questions.

Although the writer feels that the sample was representative of a typical Singapore candidature in a typical year, she cannot demonstrate this and as such cautions against over-generalizations and recommends that the present study be read in its context.

In the present study it appears that spatial visualization skills are important to the learning of mathematics. Among the Singapore pupils it was found that girls were lacking in such skills and the issue does warrant attention. Would teaching girls and boys separately, using sex-biased examples and methods of instruction, match the performance of the two sexes on parallel sex-biased problems which contain a spatial element? Does the upbringing of children in most Asian homes, where boys enjoy more attention from their parents and more time and freedom in outdoor unsupervised activities as compared to girls, contribute to the nurturing of spatial visualization skills?

In a society like Singapore's where academic excellence, more so in the sciences than the arts, is viewed as success in life, parental influence on pupils' performance in mathematics as well as sex-role differentiation through sex-typed leisure activities, subject preferences and career intentions may well be worth investigating.

For a general study on sex differences in mathematics attainment of Singapore pupils (in a selective type of education system) nothing can be more desirable than to investigate it by following the progress and performance of a sample of boys and girls over the period of their secondary or primary to secondary school education, with built in tests for cognitive and affective variables.

REFERENCES

Benford, M. (1976) The ultimate fallacy. *Times Educational Supplement*, 29 October.
Cable, J. (1976) A society for the preservation of fractions. *Mathematics in School*, 5 (4).
Department of Education and Science (1980) *Mathematical Development*. London: HMSO.
Driver, G. (1980) How West Indians do better at school (especially the girls). *New Society,* 51 (902), 111–114.
Fennema, E. and Sherman, J. (1977) Sex-related differences in mathematics achievement, spatial visualization and affective factors. *American Educational Research Journal*, 14 (1), 51–71.
Jones, D.A. (1973) *An Investigation of the Differences Between Boys and Girls During the Formative Years in the Methods Used to Solve Mathematical Problems*. Unpublished M Phil thesis. University of London, Institute of Education.
Kerlinger, F.N. (1964) *Foundations of Behavioural Research*. New York: Holt, Rinehart & Winston.
Maccoby, E.E. and Jacklin, C.N. (1974) *The Psychology of Sex Differences*. Stanford, CA: Stanford University Press.
National Assessment of Educational Progress (1975) Males dominate in educational success. *NAEP Newsletter*, 8, 5.
Sharma, S. and Meighan, R. (1980) Schooling and sex roles: the cases of GCE 'O' level mathematics. *British Journal of Sociology of Education*, 1 (2), 193–205.
Wood, R. (1977) Cable's comparison factor: is this where girls' trouble starts? *Maths in School,* 6 (4), 18–21.
Youngman, M.B. (1975) *Programmed Methods for Multivariate Data*. University of Nottingham, School of Education.
Youngman, M.B. (1976) *Programmed Methods for Multivariate Data*, 5. University of Nottingham School of Education.

Chapter 11

True or False: Primary School Girls Do Badly at Maths

Evangelie Tressou-Milonas

During the school year 1985–1986 I conducted research concerning the possibilities of applying SMP 7–13, an English method of teaching maths, in Greek primary schools. The main objective of the research was to establish if and under which conditions such an individualized system could be applied. Children's positive reactions to the new approach and changes of attitude towards maths, as well as progress in the subject, would support an argument for the application of SMP 7–13 as the main teaching approach or as a supplement to the existing programme and teaching method.

The sample for the research consisted of children in the second class of three primary schools in Thessaloniki, more or less representative of three social strata (urban, working-class and rural). The sample was very small (21 boys and 28 girls in all) but unfortunately the means and conditions under which the research was conducted did not allow for a bigger sample, more representative, that is, of the city population.[1]

During the research the children were given various attainment tests and towards the end of the school year they were asked to complete a questionnaire reporting their experience from working on a completely different system through a totally novel teaching method.

The size of the sample, the duration and the nature of the research are such that we could not possibly draw definite conclusions. Nevertheless, the children's answers both to the questionnaire and the attainment test, as well as their reactions and comments during the lessons, offered some ground for observations concerning the children's performance and general attitude towards maths.

THE GIRLS—THEIR ATTITUDE TO MATHS

Classroom observation

An important feature of SMP 7–13 is that it engages pupils in a number of domestic activities, such as weighing, measuring, shopping, traditionally considered feminine rather than masculine. Another characteristic of the method is that the content as well as the illustrations on the cards are carefully designed to avoid sex-role discrimination. Thus they avoid the suggestion of cultural norms or gender stereotypes.

We observed during the lessons that girls as well as boys found maths an exciting task and were all very eager to be involved in the activities required by the cards. The girls felt confident and very much at ease with most of the topics. Furthermore, as the pupils were allowed to proceed at their own pace, the girls made a conscious effort to surpass the boys.

The fact that SMP 7–13 allows for children to work on their own, in pairs or in small groups reduces the need for the teacher's intervention. Even when it was necessary for the researcher to interfere and explain, this was done on a person-to-person basis. Situations where a question was addressed to the whole class and one pupil was called upon to answer were very rare. Thus the timidity and fear of ridicule in case of erroneous answers usually characteristic of girls were overcome as almost all questions and answers were expressed individually.

Finally, the researcher's sex might have positively influenced the girls' progress. Several of them went so far as to state that they would like to become mathematicians when they grew up.

The questionnaire

The majority of the girls replied on the questionnaire that they would like to spend more time in doing maths from the cards. No differences were observed in the children's views regarding the topics they liked most, the ones that caused them difficulties or those elements of the teaching material that attracted them more.

In all three schools no serious differences were detected in the attitudes of boys and girls towards maths. Both boys and girls exhibited the same enthusiasm or faced the same difficulties on certain topics; they showed common preferences for particular pieces of apparatus or certain activities. There were girls as well as boys who burst out crying because of their inability to understand a concept or answer a question. Both boys and girls appeared reluctant when asked to work on a topic they were not interested in. On the other hand, they worked hard and with zeal on topics they liked, or involved the use of attractive apparatus or allowed them to co-operate with a fellow pupil they favoured. The girls felt as free to move around in the classroom or go out to the school-yard as boys and they were as vivid and active as their male peers.

Finally, the children's answers to the questionnaire suggest that at this age children's positive or negative responses to a particular topic depend on the attractiveness of the topic.

THE GIRLS' PERFORMANCE IN THE GIVEN TESTS

The test results indicated that in two of the three schools the girls did better than the boys at the given tests. Thus in the 41st school (17 girls, 6 boys) the percentage of correct answers was 90.05 per cent for the girls and 88.25 per cent for the boys. In the Aghia Triada school (8 girls, 7 boys) the percentage was 81.62 per cent and 79.45 per cent correspondingly. Only in the 9th school (3 girls, 8 boys) were the percentages inverted and the boys' scores higher than the girls' (76.47 per cent for the girls and 81.98 per cent for the boys).

The erroneous answers also include the unanswered questions. It should perhaps be mentioned here that in two of the three schools the percentage of the girls who did not answer all the questions was bigger than the corresponding percentage of the boys. Thus in the rural (Aghia Triada) school it was 8.82 per cent for the girls and 4.41 per cent for the boys, whereas for the working-class (9th) school the percentages were 13.73 per cent for the girls and 4.42 per cent for the boys. In the 41st school (the urban school), however, the percentages of unanswered questions were 1.21 per cent for the girls and 4.41 per cent for the boys. In conclusion, out of all the children participating (28 girls, 21 boys) the girls were more successful than the boys (84.94 per cent for the girls and 82.14 per cent for the boys) but they also left more questions unanswered (5.98 per cent for the girls as opposed to 4.41 per cent for the boys).

The sample (55 children in all) was undoubtedly very small. Moreover, only 49 of the children took the test while the remaining 6 children were excluded for various reasons.[2] Nevertheless the fact that the sample represented three diverse areas of the city allows for certain general observations.

1. Girls at this age, 7 + , do not seem to be inferior to boys as far as their competence in maths is concerned.
2. The girls of certain social classes (for instance, working-class and rural) hesitate more than the boys when asked to produce an answer about which they are not absolutely positive.
3. It appears that for children of working-class families maths is seen as a more appropriate subject for boys.
4. On the contrary the upper middle class girls seem to progress at maths more than their male peers, and moreover they appear bolder and more positive about their knowledge of things.

The concepts found difficult by either girls or boys were certainly not the same for all three schools. The most difficult subjects for girls are highlighted in Figure 11.1, with the number of each particular exercise on the horizontal axis, and the degree of success on the vertical. The subjects of the exercises in question are: ex. 27: problem with coins; ex. 37: time (they are asked to find the time one hour later than a clock shows); ex. 58 and 59: the difference between two given numbers. It should be noted here that exercise 27 was one of the most difficult exercises for boys as well (see below).

Figure 11.1 clearly indicates a superiority of the 41st school girls as opposed to their counterparts in the other two schools[3] and also a gradual decline of the girls' ability over the three schools (starting from the highest success rate of the 41st school girls and ending up with the lowest attainment of the 9th school girls). By comparison Figure 11.2 shows that boys faced difficulties in more exercises than girls. The most difficult questions encountered by boys were: ex. 19: about fractions; ex. 25: counting up by four on the number line; ex. 27, 42 and 44: the use of coins; ex. 52: a whole turn; ex. 61: pictorial forms.[4]

From Figure 11.2 it becomes apparent that the boys of the 41st school were not the ones who encountered the least difficulties, even if the percentage of correct

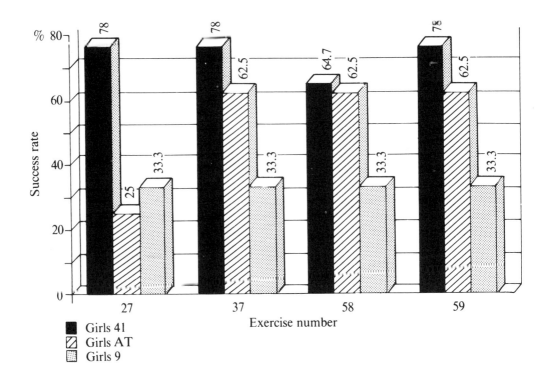

Figure 11.1   *The most difficult exercises for girls.*

answers they produced (88.25 per cent) was considerably higher than the corresponding percentage of the boys of the other two schools.[5]

One might therefore claim that the social class the children belong to probably influences their relation and their attitude towards mathematics, and moreover that it affects girls in a different way from boys. As far as the subjects in which the girls seemed to lag behind the boys (and vice versa) it was rather difficult for us to draw firm conclusions. It would be safer for the particular research if the subjects which caused the most difficulties to the majority of boys and girls were pointed out. To suggest topics at which girls are better than boys or the opposite was rather beyond the scope of the present study.

CONCLUSIONS

In summary, one could claim that during this small-scale research no differences in attitudes to maths were detected between boys and girls. The girls were as willing to do maths as the boys. They participated in the various activities with zeal and they managed perfectly well whatever they tackled.

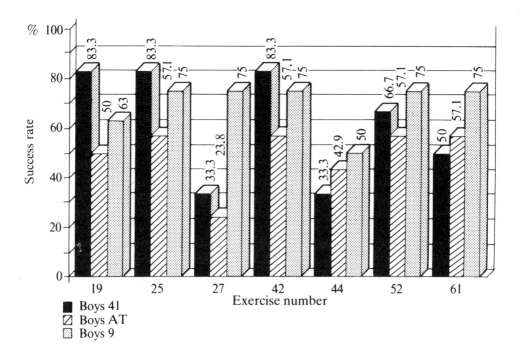

Figure 11.2   *The most difficult exercises for boys.*

Both boys and girls favoured particular subjects, not necessarily the same. The children's preferences seemed to be influenced by either the facility of the exercises or the appearance of the card. If, that is, a card included pictures particularly liked by the children or it involved the use of apparatus the children found attractive, it became a favourite. In short the girls' performance on the whole was better than that of the boys, although the percentage of questions unanswered by the girls was much higher.

Furthermore, a relation was detected between the social class the children belonged to and their competence in maths as well as their reaction to a new work scheme.

Finally, once more it should be stressed that the limitations posed by the research design only allow for certain assumptions, which simply confirm the conclusions reached by previous researchers on the subject.

NOTES

(1)   The design of the research demanded teaching which was carried out by the researcher herself twice a week for each class in combination with their Greek maths curriculum.
(2)   Four pupils of the 9th primary school (the working-class school) were practically illiterate. These particular pupils did not work from the SMP cards but used a different approach. Two of the 41st school children did not take the test; one of them took little part in the card work due to special psychological problems and the other worked at such a slow pace that the material covered by the end of the school year did not qualify her to take the test.
(3)   It would be difficult to draw conclusions regarding the 9th school girls' abilities and to compare them to the abilities of the girls in the other two schools since here the percentage 33.3 per cent represents the attainment level of one girl only.
(4)   It should be noted here that the questions on the use of coins caused particular difficulties, not only to the boys but to the girls as well, the difference being that they were not common to all the girls of the three schools.
(5)   The test scores achieved by the children (boys and girls) of the 41st (the urban area) school were the highest of all three schools.

BIBLIOGRAPHY

Assessment of Performance Unit (APU) (1980) *Mathematical Development Primary Survey Report No. 1*. London: HMSO.
Badger, M. (1981) Why aren't girls better at maths? A review of research. *Educational Research*, **24** (1), 11.
Burton, L. (ed.) (1986) *Girls into Mathematics Can Go*. London: Cassell.
Evans, D. (1977) *Mathematics: Friend or Foe?* London: George Allen & Unwin.
Fennema, E. (1985) Explaining sex-related differences in mathematics: theoretical models. *Educational Studies in Mathematics*, **16** (3), 303.
Galton, M. and Simon, B. (eds) (1980) *Inside the Primary Classroom*. London: Routledge & Kegan Paul.
Kaplan, B. and Plake, B. (1982) Sex differences in mathematics: difference in basic logical skills? *Educational Studies*, **8** (8), 31.
Millman, V. (1983) Reducing sex role differentiation in schools. A schools council project. *Primary Education Review*, Summer.
Shuard, H. (1982) The sex factor. *Junior Education*, November, 9.
Sutherland, M. (1981) *Sex Bias in Education*. London: Basil Blackwell.
Walden, R. and Walkerdine, V. (1982) *Girls and Mathematics: The Early Years*. London: Bedford Way Papers 8, Institute of Education, University of London.
Walden, R. and Walkerdine, V. (1985) *Girls and Mathematics: From Primary to Secondary Schooling*. London: Bedford Way Papers 24, Institute of Education, University of London.
Whyte, J. (1983) How girls learn to be losers. *Primary Education Review*, Summer, 5.

Chapter 12

Graduate Education in the Mathematical Sciences: Factors Influencing Women and Men

Joanne Rossi Becker

The small number of women in science and engineering in the USA has been well documented (NSF, 1986). Although more women are pursuing undergraduate degrees in the mathematical sciences, they continue to comprise a relatively small percentage of those earning advanced degrees in those fields. In 1983, the most recent year for which data are available, women in the USA earned 44, 35, and 17 per cent of the Bachelor, Master and Doctoral degrees in mathematics. In computer science, the analogous figures were 36, 28, and 13 per cent (degrees conferred, 1985; Syverson and Forster, 1983).

Concern about removing educational and career barriers to women in the sciences has led to a number of studies aimed at identifying factors related to a woman's choice of a scientific career. Only recently has research focused on women currently enrolled in a graduate programme, or recently graduated from one. Few of these studies targeted women in the mathematical sciences exclusively. Computer science, a field with a growing number of graduates and increasing influence in society, is a new discipline which nevertheless attracts a disproportionate number of men, yet has received little research attention. Information about factors influencing women to pursue advanced study in mathematics and computer science would help us design programmes and interventions to encourage women to attend graduate school in those disciplines.

BACKGROUND

Helson (1976) studied men and women PhDs in mathematics to determine if there were relationships between psychological variables and creativity in mathematics. Women showed similar motivation to engage in mathematics as men. The major differences between the genders related to social functioning: the men were assertive, confident, and comfortable in their social world; the women were non-assertive, lacked confidence, and were less comfortable in their social world.

Luchins (1976) distributed a questionnaire to 350 female and 52 male members of the Association for Women in Mathematics to determine factors that encouraged or discouraged female mathematicians. Scherrei and McNamara (1981) interviewed 25 women (none in mathematics) in the early stages of their careers in science. Combined findings from these studies indicated that an early interest in mathematics or science was almost universal among these women. The mathematicians felt that women were discouraged from pursuing careers in mathematics, particularly by society's sex-typing of mathematics as a male domain. Counsellors were found to be more of a hindrance than a help to women in making career decisions. Contact with successful female role-models was a very positive experience for a number of women in both studies.

Zappert and Stansbury (1984) and Stansbury (1986) reported on results of a survey of men and women in graduate programmes in science, engineering and medicine at Stanford University. About nine per cent of the students in the sample were in the mathematical sciences. These studies report that men and women experience different pressures and blocks in their graduate careers. Despite similar academic backgrounds, the women felt less competent and confident about their abilities. Women were found to be more sensitive to supportive features of the academic environment, particularly relations with the advisor.

Becker (1984) reported on in-depth interviews conducted with ten graduate students in mathematics, six male and four female, to identify factors influencing them to pursue a graduate degree in mathematics. Male and female graduate students expressed similar reasons for liking mathematics: its logical nature, its problem-solving aspects, its objectivity, and its creative nature. Most developed an interest in and love for mathematics in elementary school. Differences between men and women were found in the process of deciding to attend graduate school, in their confidence in their mathematical abilities, and in their career aspirations. The women seemed to need strong encouragement from at least one person, usually a teacher, to decide to try graduate school. The relative lack of confidence of the women was reflected in their career goals. Both men and women generally wanted to teach; but the women's sights were set at a lower level or toward a non-research institution.

These studies have provided some information about factors that might continue to influence women to choose a mathematical career. The purpose of this study was to expand the sample from the Becker (1984) study to include graduate students in computer science to determine if previous findings are corroborated.

METHODOLOGY

This study was conducted in two phases at two different institutions, called here East University and West University. East University is the same institution in which the previous study (Becker, 1984) was conducted. In the current study, eight graduate students in computer science (a separate department from mathematics) volunteered to be interviewed. The author spoke at a mandatory meeting the first day of school to solicit participants; a follow-up letter was sent to all graduate students, resulting in the eight volunteers. These interviews were conducted in 1983.

In 1985, a similar procedure was used to get participants in both mathematics and computer science at West University; here both disciplines are in the same department. At West, an additional 13 participants were interviewed, 5 in mathematics and 8 in computer science.

An interview approach was used to provide in-depth information about the dynamics of educational and career choices. The audiotaped interviews focused on educational, family, and work background; interests in mathematics/computers and when they developed; reasons for pursuing a graduate degree; influences on that decision; and long-range career goals. Qualitative methods of analysis were used to ascertain patterns of responses and categorize them into a taxonomy.

RESULTS

Description of sample

East and West Universities differed in other than geographical ways. As stated above, at East the mathematics and computer science fields are in two different departments. This seems to have influenced the programmes in computer science; there are Masters' degrees offered in computer science or computer information science. Degrees may have a large component of coursework in other departments, such as business. The programme caters to students who do not have undergraduate background in computers by offering a special one-year catch-up course in computer science. Also, the graduate degrees do not have substantial mathematics requirements. East is a large public research institution which offers Doctoral degrees.

In contrast, at West, mathematics and computer science are in the same department. The Masters' degree courses are more highly mathematized; a substantial amount of upper division mathematics is required to enter a graduate programme. West is also a public institution, but does not offer Doctoral degrees in either mathematics or computer science.

Of the eight informants at East University, four were male and four female. Their ages ranged from 24 to 55 years; only two students, one male and one female, were pursuing a graduate degree immediately after receiving a Bachelors' degree. Their educational backgrounds varied considerably. All the men came from a technological background (degrees in engineering and mathematics, one with a Masters' in mechanical engineering). Two of the women had mathematics backgrounds, one a Bachelors' and one through a PhD. One woman had a PhD in German; the other had a Bachelors' in classics and a Masters' in education. Only two of the informants, both male, intended to pursue a PhD in computer science.

At West University, five students were in mathematics (three male, two female) and eight in computer science (four male, four female). One female was Asian. Their ages again had a large range: 24–48 years. Of the mathematics students, all but one had undergraduate degrees in mathematics; the one exception had a physics degree. In contrast, the computer science sample included only two undergraduate degrees in computer science, reflecting the newness of the discipline. The rest had degrees in mathematics, a science, or engineering. The difference in programmes in the two institutions clearly has an impact on what kind of students can pursue graduate degrees. At West, one male in computer science intended to pursue a PhD in the field elsewhere; two mathematics students, one male and one female, have gone on to a PhD programme at other prestigious universities.

The family backgrounds of informants defy generalizations. The only common factor to most was a value for education and encouragement to attend college. However, two women were discouraged by family from even attending college.

Patterns of responses

Patterns that emerged in the responses from the informants were grouped into major categories. Contrasts between mathematics and computer science informants will be discussed within each category. In the quotes provided to illustrate a pattern, the following codes are used: R (researcher); F (female); M (male); Ma (mathematics); Cs (computer science). A numeral will be used after the gender code to signify a specific informant of that gender. For example, F-3 (Ma) will stand for the third female cited; she is a mathematics student.

When their interests developed

Nearly all of the informants expressed an interest in and liking for mathematics or science in the elementary or junior high school years. Having a teacher who was really a mathematics teacher seemed to make a difference in how the subject was taught which piqued the interest of students.

R:	Can you reflect on when you started liking mathematics?
M-1 (Ma):	Yeah, when I was in seventh grade. I used not to like it.
R:	Why was that?
M-1 (Ma):	I remember long division, I hated doing long division. . . . Then when I was in seventh grade that's what really did it. I had this teacher that was really good. She did a lot of non-traditional things with math.
F-1 (Cs):	Well, I've always liked math, and I guess what I really needed was just, you know, somebody just behind me pushing me a little more.
M-2 (Cs):	I remember that through the first six grades in school, school really didn't have very much interest for me. It was all just a bunch of drudgery as far as I was concerned. . . . In seventh grade I took algebra. . . . All of a sudden it was interesting. From then on I majored in math.

Even those students who did not have a technological background seemed to like mathematics early in their education. The informant who had a PhD in German actually had been a mathematics major before switching to German.

Why they like mathematics/computer science

Certainly one important reason people like a subject is that they are good at it. This factor was mentioned again and again by both mathematics and computer science majors. Although there did not appear to be gender differences in the reasons for liking mathematics/computer science, there were clear differences between majors in the two fields.

A very appealing aspect of mathematics is its problem-solving nature. Students appreciate the challenge of trying to solve a mathematical problem, and compare this to solving crossword puzzles or playing a game. One has certain assumptions and rules, and through logic, can solve the puzzle.

M-3 (Ma):   . . . the actual learning process is fun in itself and it's like a game almost. You start out with certain sets of assumptions and you build the problem and you're creating this fixed structure which is just amazing it holds together. I mean the whole thing just holds together and you get these results that are consistent. The whole thing is like a game that's fascinating to me.

F-2 (Ma):   My love, my true love has always been logic. From the minute that I first took a logic class I said, this is what I want to do.

The appeal of the structure of mathematics, closely related to its logical nature, was also of importance. To these students, the structure exemplified the beauty of mathematics.

F-3 (Ma):   Mathematics is a language and the proofs a manipulation of language. It's just generation of transformation of a different kind of language when you think of it. Except there's no rule when you stop transforming like there is in language. . . . In math, apply tools to a structure in order to do things.

The objective nature of mathematics also appealed to students, as this example shows.

F-2 (Ma):   The thing that's nice about math is that's it. You do what it says right there. I like that. I also like the sense of reward. One can read a Shakespeare play for the rest of one's life and not have any kind definitive idea of what's going on.

One thing that seemed to appeal to several men, but no women, was the snob value of studying mathematics. One was doing what almost everyone else found difficult.

M-3 (Ma):   The fact that it was so intellectual and so hard and was so different really appealed to me . . . to put it bluntly, the snobbery you know, how you felt to people really stupid.

The computer science majors definitely had a different view of mathematics from the mathematics majors. These students generally did not like the abstract nature of the subject, and the emphasis on proving theorems from a certain set of assumptions. What they liked was the usefulness of the subject, how it could be applied to solve problems. Problem-solving was definitely the most important feature of computer science to these students. The mathematics was important only so far as you could use it advantageously to solve a real problem. Still, the processes they said they used were often very mathematical in nature, and they stressed even more the appeal of knowing you are right because the programme works.

M-4 (Cs):   The reason I said debugging as the first thing is that because that's sort of the most obvious place where you do problem-solving, because you have a very clear-cut problem, what's wrong with the program, and a very clear-cut path, very clear-cut whether you've fixed it or not. . . . I definitely like programming. I think it boils down to I like solving problems.

M-5 (Cs):   I see mathematicians as very useful tool builders. But I see that mathematicians often forget that they're building tools.

M-6 (Cs):   I like to be able to use it as a tool in math sometimes and I think from the math teachers I've seen there has been some hesitancy about doing that. . . . I mean it's nice to have a program that just sits there and looks elegant but, like to write something that can do something useful.

F-4 (Cs):   All the other things in the world, you know the job's out of your control, . . . but in programs everything is under your control. You know exactly what you want to do and you should be able to make it do what you want it to do.

F-5 (Cs):   It's like problem-solving. It's like crossword puzzles. The clues are all there and at first it doesn't seem to make any sense but if you look at it a while it begins to make sense.

F-6 (Cs):   I like the, not really that it's a game, but that kind of mentality to it.

F-7 (Cs):   You've got that feedback, I need that response. And I get that from computers. It's playing games. It's like jigsaw puzzles and scrabble and all those sort of things.

F-8 (Cs):   The problem is solved because you see the output. . . . It's very concrete, you can put your finger on it. . . . Abstract mathematics has always eluded me to some extent. It seems to me that mathematicians are often proving things which are obvious. . . . Computer science says, I can prove it because my machine works using it.

Academic preparation

Nearly every informant, except the oldest ones, had been involved in some special programme in mathematics or science as early as junior high school. Many had taken algebra either one or two years early because of being identified as gifted in mathematics; several of these students then studied through calculus in high school. One student studied junior high mathematics from the SMSG programme, which stressed the structural aspects of mathematics which appealed to her. Another woman attended an all-female parochial school in which students were particularly encouraged in mathematics and science. A third woman was in an NSF-sponsored summer programme in junior high which involved her in computer programming. Several informants had been in a maths club or on a maths team in high school. Even the computer science majors who had non-technical undergraduate majors had studied a substantial amount of mathematics in high school; this perhaps helps account for their ability to succeed when going back to a mathematical field after many years.

Ten of the computer science graduate students had had little or no computer science background when they began their programmes. Although willing to admit the need to work hard at being a student again, none of the men expressed any difficulty adjusting to the level of coursework they had undertaken. However, several of the women did find difficulty adjusting to being a student after a gap of some years. The women were more likely to feel isolated in graduate school, or to find conflict between family demands and the time demands needed to write successful programs. Several women (at both institutions) felt they were not always taken seriously by faculty members. One recounted going into a faculty member's office with a male student to ask a question, and being ignored throughout the conversation. Another was distressed by professors' inability to tell her and one other older woman apart, although they bore little resemblance to each other. These students persisted and received their degrees, but one must wonder if others were discouraged who might have achieved a graduate degree.

Why they chose graduate school

A large part of the interviews centred on factors that influenced the decision to attend graduate school in mathematics or computer science. Some differences emerged here between the men and women. More of the men than women, in both disciplines, seemed to have a clear reason for applying to graduate school. The women seemed less sure of their goals and less certain of their ability to succeed (see categories below as well). However, it was surprising how many of the informants had never made real clear decisions about graduate school.

F-1 (Cs): I said, well I'll apply and see what happens, and honestly, I really did not think I would get accepted.

F-9 (Cs): But sort of a lot of decisions have been made not by me carefully thinking through all the options but just sort of jumping on what's available.

Contrast these comments with a typical male response.

M-7 (Cs): Well, I had always wanted to do more than just get a Bachelors'. It was a choice really as to field.

Career goals

One clear difference between the mathematics and computer science majors related to practical economic goals. Those in a graduate programme in computer science were well aware of the numbers of jobs available and the high starting salaries. One reason so few intended to pursue a PhD is that they did not view that degree as buying one much beyond a Masters' in terms of salary or opportunity. The PhD is for those who want to teach at the university level, and they make less than a computer scientist in industry who only has a Bachelors' degree.

In contrast, all of the mathematics students had a career goal of teaching. Those in a Masters' programme only wanted to teach at a junior college; those planning a PhD hoped for a university teaching position. These students seemed to have very little idea of what they could do besides teach. They loved mathematics, and liked teaching, so it seemed natural to combine these interests. One difference found between men and women is that the women had high school teaching credentials (they had been encouraged to do this), but only one man had such a credential. Thus, the original career goals of the women were to teach at the high school level; they found that unsatisfying, so sought other options.

For the computer science majors, one clear gender difference involved the desire not to use the degree in defence-related work. Only one man expressed that concern. The rest seemed more interested in the intellectual challenge of a job than in its area of application. Somehow this desire to avoid defence work led more of the women to a career choice of teaching; again, most students had little idea of what they could do with their degrees, despite all the publicity about the computer field.

F-9 (Cs): I was very active in some of the social movements, and interested in saving the world from poverty, war, and in industry, that might have something to do with war-related things, so I sort of didn't want to work in industry, which left teaching, as far as I was concerned.

Five of the women but only one man had an immediate goal to teach once finished with the degree. Additionally, one man and one woman intended to pursue teaching after working a few years in industry to make money and gain practical experience. They admitted not knowing if they could leave a lucrative job for a lower-paying teaching position in the future.

Encouragement and discouragement

There were several factors grouped into this category which showed gender differences. In general, the women were influenced more by 'significant others' than were the men (or at least they were willing to admit it). Although most participants mentioned family as influencing their decisions, this influence seemed more important to the women. And several women, but no men, were discouraged by family from even attending college.

F-4 (Cs): I can't say they really pressed me to go into whatever area, but my parents, and my brothers and sisters always let me know what they think is good for me. I think I want to go into music. . . . But I know that they would be very unhappy.

F-6 (Cs): My parents weren't going to pay for college for a girl, so I had to work, not full-time but pretty heavy for two years.

M-8 (Ma):   It was just always assumed that I would go to college.

All but one woman, but only three men, mentioned at least one teacher who was a special influence. For many of the informants, this special teacher was in junior high or high school; s/he was influential mainly because of the way s/he taught mathematics, making it fun, interesting, and challenging as it never before had been. Many of the women had more than one important teacher, one before college, and one or more in college who particularly encouraged them to major in mathematics/computer science and to consider graduate school.

M-1 (Ma):   She, I don't actually remember exactly, it was sort of like more puzzle type things and we used to have these team games. It was enjoyable for the first time. . . . Maybe that pinpoints what happened with my seventh grade teacher. She emphasized intuitive understanding, coming to your own conclusions. . . . If I hadn't had these few teachers in junior high, for sure I would never have been in math.

F-9 (Cs):   I didn't initiate any of that, I had, again had one professor in particular and another one, that sort of was encouraging me to continue. Sort of a cheer-leader, kept telling me I should go on [to graduate school].

F-2 (Ma):   I got an enormous amount of encouragement throughout my experience at State from the people in the math department. When I would say things like I said to you, 'Well, if I were brilliant I would have gone into logic' they would say, 'Who told you you weren't?'. . . Boost my confidence.

Not only individuals but also institutions as a whole may encourage or discourage students. Although the women had strong memories of support and discouragement, the men recalled much less encouragement and no discouragement. The encouragement seemed really helpful to the women in their decisions to attend graduate school. The men seemed to be able to decide without ostensible support.
The type of experiences women, but not men, reported are illustrated by these quotes.

F-3 (Ma):   There's something about being treated like a subhuman throughout high school because you're good in math . . . There wasn't really that much overt discrimination, but it just seems that the idea that the men are more serious students, it's just always underneath there.

F-2 (Ma):   A common sort of thing to happen, if we go in, if a woman goes in with a man to talk to an instructor about some question she, not necessarily he, is working on, the instructor almost universally answers the man with whom the woman went.

F-6 (Cs):   One of the reasons I ended up minoring in education was because that's where all the girls were. My physics class was 500 people, and there were only two girls . . .

R: How did that feel, being such a minority?

F-6:   There were a lot of disadvantages to it. Some of the older professors didn't think I belonged there [engineering] so they were very degrading at times. . . . But the worst part was the attitude of the other students. I found I was shunned a lot.

Three women at West University ended up in the computer science department instead of computer engineering because they perceived a more supportive environment. The computer engineering department was described as almost totally male, faculty and students, and not a place they felt comfortable. They felt the faculty really did not want them around. The mathematics and computer science department has many more women around, although they do not teach graduate courses. The milieu of the department seemed important to the women, less so to the men, perhaps because they felt they really belonged there.

Self-confidence

Some of the experiences described above may contribute to the gender difference found for both mathematics and computer science majors in this category. The women generally had less confidence in their abilities in their field; this seemed to contribute to lack of ambition for a doctoral degree. The men expressed confidence in their abilities, and usually denied ever having any difficulties in coursework or other aspects of their graduate programme. The women were much more likely spontaneously to mention difficult points in their programmes, and their coping mechanisms. There was no evidence from grades or degree attainment that the women were less successful; they just seemed to feel that they were, as illustrated by these comments.

F-2 (Ma):   Every now and again I think that maybe I am a little smart. But I sure pulled the wool over their eyes. . . . having to perform these acrobatics so that they won't find out that I'm really stupid. I do consider myself to be just a hack. . . . If I were brilliant then it would be easy for me.

R: Do you think most people who are PhDs in logic are brilliant?

F-2 (Ma):   At least they're cocky. If not brilliant, real cocky.

R: Do you feel like you have a pretty good background to go on for your doctorate?

F-3 (Ma):   No. I'm still not good enough in algebra. . . . I never remember as much of what I study as I feel I should. But I think of all that I've studied now, I have a solid undergraduate background. [Note: this student had just completed her Masters' orals.]

M-3 (Ma):   I just did very very well in everything. I mean in the math sense I wasn't pushed, I was alone, I always managed to get an A, I always managed to do the best in the class. It was just never really a problem.

R: Was it difficult for you coming back [to school] after having been out for 12 years?

M-11 (Cs):   I didn't find it difficult at all . . . I already knew that I would do well at school.

F-1 (Cs):   Cause the Masters' degree for me has really been a struggle, and I've told so many people, if I ever mention getting a PhD, please knock me over the head . . . Because it's really been tough, and I guess I want more out of life.

F-9 (Cs):   I'd still be a graduate student [in mathematics] if Dr L had not said it's enough. Here, write it up, and quit telling me it's not enough.

CONCLUSIONS

Male and female graduate students in both mathematics and computer science expressed similar reasons for liking their disciplines. A feature common to both disciplines was the problem-solving. That which is most difficult for the majority of students is what is attractive to those specializing in a mathematical science. Interest in the problem-solving began early for most informants, usually by junior high school. A key difference between the two disciplines was apparent in the type of mathematics they liked. Those in pure mathematics really enjoyed the abstract nature of the subject and writing proofs from a set of assumptions and previous theorems. Those in computer science had little appreciation for the most abstract mathematics; they saw mathematics as a tool to help them solve application problems. This difference parallels the often-cited one between scientists and engineers.

The men in this sample seemed to have stronger self-motivation to attend graduate school than did the women. The women seemed to need strong encouragement from at least one person to try graduate study. More of the women reported both encouragement and discouragement in their educational careers. These experiences perhaps contributed to a relatively lower level of confidence in the women than the men. This lack of confidence is reflected in their career aspirations, and perhaps helps account for the need for some external validation of their abilities to achieve advanced degrees.

A small number of women in this study returned successfully for a Masters' degree in computer science without a mathematically oriented undergraduate background. The fact that this is possible without taking a large number of undergraduate mathematics and computer science courses seems to be a well-kept secret. If the potential population for Masters' degrees in computer science were to include people with social science or humanities degrees, many more women would be eligible for retraining. Unfortunately, this is not true in mathematics, where a Bachelors' degree in mathematics or a related field seems crucial.

The factors influencing students to pursue graduate degrees in the mathematical sciences which have been identified here suggest ways colleges and universities could encourage more women to attend graduate school. The pool of undergraduates and returning women is available; a commitment to attracting and retaining women graduate students is a needed first step.

REFERENCES

Becker, J.R. (1984) The pursuit of graduate education in mathematics: factors that influence women and men. *Journal of Educational Equity and Leadership*, **4** (1), 39–53.

Degrees conferred by US Colleges and Universities, 1982–83 (1985, October) *Chronicle of Higher Education*, **31** (6), 22.

Helson, R. (1976) Subgroups of creative women in mathematics. Paper presented at the Annual Meeting of the American Association for the Advancement of Science, February.

Luchins, E.H. (1976) *Women in Mathematics: Problems of Orientation and Reorientation*. Final Report to National Science Foundation, Washington, DC.

National Science Foundation (January 1986) *Women and Minorities in Science and Engineering*. Washington, DC: NSF.

Scherrei, R.A. and McNamara, P. (1981) Factors that describe and encourage women who pursue scientific and engineering careers. Paper presented at the Mid-year conference of the American Educational Research Association, Special Interest Group-Research on Women in Education. Washington, DC, October.

Stansbury, K. (1986) The relationship of the supportiveness of the academic environment to the self-confidence and assertiveness in academic work for men and women graduate students in science and engineering. Paper presented at the Annual Meeting of the American Educational Research Association, San Francisco, April.

Syverson, P.D. and Forster, L.E. (1983) *Summary Report 1983: Doctorate Recipients from United States Universities*. Washington, DC: National Academy Press.

Zappert, L.T. and Stansbury, K. (1984) *In the Pipeline: A Comparative Analysis of Men and Women in Graduate Progams in Science, Engineering and Medicine at Stanford University*. Palo Alto, CA: Stanford University.

Chapter 13

Where Have the Mathematicians Gone in New Zealand?

Prudence Purser and Helen Wily

Is the number of mathematics graduates increasing?
Are more women graduating in mathematics?
What are the destinations of mathematics graduates?
Are women advancing to the higher degrees?
What occupations do mathematics graduates enter?
Where are the future mathematics teachers?

These are some of the questions that are addressed in this chapter. The responses to them are of value to educationalists, to employers and to those requiring the specialized knowledge and skills of the highly qualified graduate in mathematics.

The information used is from the annual graduate survey conducted by each university. Each year's survey covers the period 1 June to the following 31 May. Figures for 1972/73 therefore refer to those who graduated from 1 June 1972 to 31 May 1973. There is always a very high response to this questionnaire and this establishes the validity of the figures used in this report.

In this study, the data used are only of those graduates whose first major is categorized by the Graduate Employment Survey as mathematics. This category includes degrees in pure and applied mathematics, statistics and systems. This does not include the many students who study mathematics but for whom mathematics is not the major part of their degree. It should also be noted that these figures include not only younger graduates taking up their first permanent occupation but also older graduates who may not be entering employment for the first time.

IS THE NUMBER OF MATHEMATICS GRADUATES INCREASING?

Table 13.1 includes overseas students who have been educated in New Zealand. It must also be noticed that there is a duplication of figures, as a student who graduates with a first degree may reappear as a statistic after they have completed a further degree. Hence the total number of individuals graduating in mathematics is fewer than the table indicates.

Table 13.1. *Graduates in mathematics 1972//73–1985/86*

Years	Doctoral		Diploma		BSocSc		B(Hon)SocSc MSocSc		BSc		B(Hon)Sc		MSc		BBusAdmin BFoodSc BEng B(Hon)Bus Admin		Totals		ALL
	M	F	M	F	M	F	M	F	M	F	M	F	M	F	M	F	M	F	
1972/73	4	0	3	2	14	11	3	2	165	43	29	—	14	1	0	0	232	62	294
1973/74	2	0	3	1	13	12	4	1	144	55	22	15	15	1	3	2	206	87	293
1974/75	2	1	5	0	26	16	4	1	149	54	22	7	22	3	1	0	230	82	312
1975/76	2	0	7	4	13	17	1	5	117	39	28	5	20	8	4	5	192	83	275
1976/77	5	0	3	7	18	20	3	2	110	31	18	6	15	3	1	0	173	69	242
1977/78	4	1	7	1	15	15	3	3	115	52	27	8	18	3	4	0	193	83	276
1978/79	7	0	6	2	20	8	4	4	119	42	31	10	16	3	2	0	205	69	274
1979/80	5	1	3	3	15	17	3	0	120	40	22	3	16	3	2	2	186	69	255
1980/81	0	0	4	4	14	15	6	0	100	43	25	5	13	2	3	0	165	69	234
1981/82	2	0	4	6	17	12	0	4	100	51	21	11	18	3	2	0	164	87	251
1982/83	5	1	4	5	5	13	2	1	112	37	20	7	16	2	5	5	169	71	240
1983/84	0	0	4	1	13	11	2	1	83	32	32	6	10	3	2	1	146	57	203
1984/85	4	1	2	5	13	15	1	2	114	56	22	5	22	1	2	1	180	86	266
1985/86	7	0	1	4	13	9	3	1	104	52	20	5	6	4	3	0	157	75	232

Table 13.1 shows that the number of graduates in mathematics, though fluctuating, has decreased over the 14-year period. Although the number of mathematics graduates with degrees in arts and social sciences has remained steady, the number of graduates who completed a BSc in mathematics has declined. This decrease causes unease as it results in a smaller pool of talent from which to draw for higher degrees in mathematics. There was an increase of 35 per cent in the total number graduating in all subjects in 1986 compared with 1975. The proportion who graduated in mathematics for these same years fell from 4 per cent in 1975 to 2 per cent in 1986.

Are students now taking their first degree in the newer subject areas such as computing or in those areas which appear to be more vocationally orientated, such as commerce, in preference to degrees in mathematics? Whatever the reason, the supply of mathematics graduates is decreasing. The attention of those directing young people in their career choices should be drawn to the desirability of taking a mathematics degree first which gives the advantage of wide vocational options after graduation.

ARE MORE WOMEN GRADUATING IN MATHEMATICS?

Over the 14-year period, the percentage of mathematics graduates who are women ranged from 21 per cent in 1972/73 to the high point of 35 per cent in 1981/82 (the details are shown in Figure 13.1).

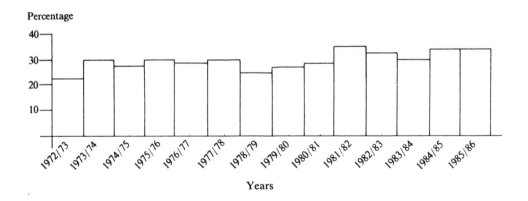

Figure 13.1 *Percentage of mathematics graduates who are women.*

There has been some obvious variation over the years but the trend does seem to be toward a slight increase in the percentage of female mathematics graduates.

It is of interest that over this 14-year period there were only 5 women who gained doctorates in mathematics compared with 49 men. The first of these women became a secondary school teacher, the second went into research, the third was not available for permanent employment, the fourth was an overseas student who returned home and the fifth was looking for employment!

WHAT ARE THE DESTINATIONS OF MATHEMATICS GRADUATES?

From the information in the graduate survey, it has been possible to identify the overseas students, the New Zealand students who continue in full-time study and those who gain employment. Those students who were not available for employment or who were still looking for a suitable job at the time of the survey have been placed in the category of 'Other' (Table 13.2).

Table 13.2. *Destinations of mathematics graduates.*

Years	Overseas students		Continuing full-time study		Employed in NZ		Other		Total	
	M	F	M	F	M	F	M	F	M	F
1972/73	29	5	105	28	74	27	24	2	232	62
1973/74	32	13	100	41	53	23	21	10	206	87
1974/75	25	8	89	41	62	24	54	9	230	82
1975/76	22	8	93	33	50	30	27	12	192	83
1976/77	16	10	96	29	41	23	20	7	173	69
1977/78	26	9	78	33	66	29	23	12	193	83
1978/79	26	9	93	23	58	24	28	13	205	69
1979/80	20	13	74	26	64	24	28	6	186	69
1980/81	20	13	53	27	65	21	27	8	165	69
1981/82	14	7	69	28	56	38	25	14	164	87
1982/83	9	4	61	26	72	32	27	9	169	71
1983/84	6	3	71	25	50	20	19	9	146	57
1984/85	15	5	59	33	75	38	31	10	180	86
1985/86	8	15	61	15	64	36	24	9	157	75

In spite of the fluctuations in the data, some patterns do emerge. To illustrate these patterns more clearly, Figure 13.2 uses four separate year periods with three or four years between each. The overall decline in the number of mathematics graduates is again evident.

The proportion of mathematics graduates who are overseas students has been falling between 1972/73 and 1983/84 with only 4 per cent of mathematics graduates in 1983/84 being from overseas. This proportion has increased again recently with the average percentage of overseas students being about 10 per cent of mathematics graduates.

There has been a slight increase, over the 14-year period, in the proportion of male mathematics graduates finding work in New Zealand. However, because of the declining number of mathematics graduates, the actual input of male mathematics graduates into the workforce has remained static. The percentage of female mathematics graduates who enter the New Zealand work force has almost always been higher than that of their male counterparts. However, unlike them, there is a slight

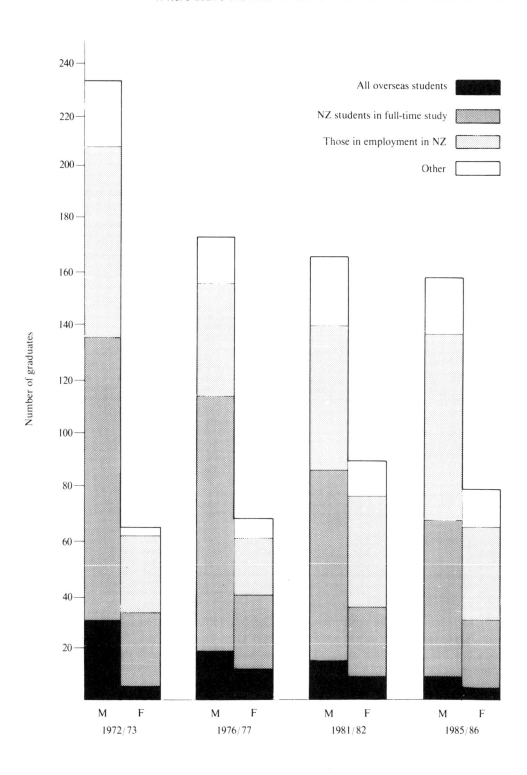

Figure 13.2 *Destination of mathematics graduates.*

increase in the number of female mathematics graduates entering the work force, as can be seen in Table 13.2.

On average, approximately 40 per cent of mathematics graduates continue in full-time study, which may be either academic or vocational. Approximately one-third of mathematics graduates are in employment within New Zealand in the six months following the completion of their degree.

ARE WOMEN ADVANCING TO THE HIGHER DEGREES?

To investigate the composition of the category of full-time study for both men and women, the figures have been looked at in more detail. The category of full-time study in Table 13.2 includes those who continue on to teacher training at either primary or secondary teachers' colleges as well as those furthering their studies at university. The figures for the teachers' colleges are listed in Table 13.6 and Table 13.3 looks only at those doing further study at a university either in New Zealand or overseas. The trends are shown in Figure 13.3.

Table 13.3 *Mathematics graduates who continue in full-time university study.*

Year of graduation	Male			Female		
	Further study in NZ	Further study overseas	% of male graduates continuing study	Further study in NZ	Further study overseas	% of female graduates continuing study
1972/73	73	6	39%	9	3	21%
1973/74	62	8	40%	15	1	22%
1974/75	63	4	33%	16	3	26%
1975/76	62	4	39%	11	3	19%
1976/77	55	11	42%	7	1	14%
1977/78	47	10	34%	15	0	20%
1978/79	57	8	36%	3	1	7%
1979/80	43	6	30%	8	1	17%
1980/81	36	6	29%	8	1	16%
1981/82	45	10	37%	10	0	13%
1982/83	46	8	34%	12	1	19%
1983/84	47	11	41%	11	1	22%
1984/85	32	13	27%	17	3	25%
1985/86	46	6	35%	8	2	17%
			$\bar{x} = 35\%$			$\bar{x} = 18\%$

It is of considerable concern to note the few female mathematics graduates who continue in full-time study towards another degree. This lower proportion of women to men has been consistent over the 14-year period surveyed and shows little sign of improvement. Without a higher degree, specialized job opportunities for women are reduced. This limiting factor should be studied further as there currently seems to be a serious shortage of highly skilled people in our technological environment.

Do women have shorter-term goals? Are they reluctant to spend more time in the role of student? Are women keen to enter the workforce? Is the university environment not conducive to women achieving the highest academic qualification of which they are capable? If female role models in university mathematics departments are necessary to

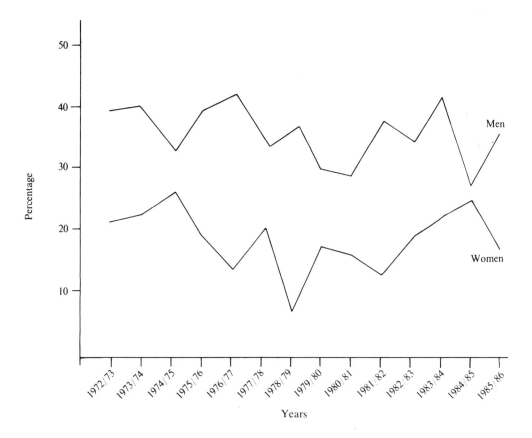

Figure 13.3 *A comparison of the proportion of male and female mathematics graduates who continue in full-time study.*

change the situation, then change here is unlikely as university lecturing is one of the specialized jobs which requires a higher degree and the situation is self-perpetuating.

WHAT OCCUPATIONS DO MATHEMATICS GRADUATES ENTER?

Table 13.4 gives a broad picture of the occupations of those mathematics graduates who weré·in permanent employment when surveyed. Generally these figures refer to their first occupation. Most graduates at that time would only recently have entered their stated employment but a few may have worked and studied concurrently and hence have been longer in their present occupation. Table 13.4 shows the totals for the 1972/73

Table 13.4. *Occupational groups of all mathematics graduates* 1972/73–1985/86.

Broad category of occupations	Occupational group	Number		
		Males	Females	Total
Armed services	Armed services personnel	18	0	18
Computing	Computer programmers, operators	86	39	125
	Methods analysts	3	0	3
	Systems analysts	28	9	37
	Operations research analysts	11	2	13
Educationalists	Lecturers (tertiary)	41	6	47
	Secondary teachers	165	82	247
	Primary, intermediate teachers	7	9	16
	Pre-primary teachers	1	0	1
	Correspondence teachers	1	2	3
	Education administrators, principals	6	4	10
Engineers	Engineers	16	1	17
	Traffic engineers	4	0	4
Finance and	Accountants	10	6	16
Commerce	Commerce, banking employees	16	7	23
	Economists	6	6	12
	Marketing and sales workers	15	3	18
	Marketing research workers	4	4	8
Insurance	Actuaries	72	27	99
	Insurance workers	11	3	14
Statisticians	Statisticians	37	42	79
	Mathematicians	4	4	8
	Social research workers	4	4	8
	Industrial engineers	3	1	4
Scientists	Physical scientists	12	0	12
	Life scientists	11	6	17
	Biometricians	9	6	15
	Technicians	13	8	21
	Field and station observers	1	0	1
	Meteorologists	10	2	12
Managers	Managers, industry and commerce	17	9	26
	Government advisory officers	11	13	24
Clerical	Clerical workers	9	8	17
Creative and	Journalists	1	0	1
Arts	Librarians	5	2	7
	Actors, musicians, etc.	6	1	7
	Photographers	1	0	1
Miscellaneous	Airline pilots, ships officers	3	1	4
	Trades workers	2	1	3
	Bus drivers, security officers	2	0	2
	Postal workers	0	1	1
		682	319	1001

to 1985/86 period. The occupations have been classified into approximately 40 groups which in turn fall into 12 main categories. Actual numbers only have been presented but the chance grand total of 1001 people makes it easy to derive the percentage distribution over the occupations.

The total number of males compared with the number of females (682 to 319) shown in Table 13.4 leads to the approximate ratio of two males to one female in employment. Hence any variation from the ratio of 2 to 1 in the number of men and women in any one employment area indicates an imbalance of representation of the two sexes in that occupation. The table was examined with this ratio in mind.

The absence of women from armed services personnel is not unexpected. The few women in some groups such as meteorologists should be noted but the marked disproportionality of 41 males to 6 females in the occupation of lecturer in a tertiary institution is disturbing. This bias in favour of the males is likely to be an outcome of women tending not to continue to higher degrees which would be a prerequisite for this type of employment. On the other hand, an approximate ratio of two to one is found in several occupations such as computer programmers, accountants, actuaries, life sciences and teachers, showing that there is an equivalent representation of men and women in these fields. The high proportion of women engaged in statistical work is of interest.

Also worthy of comment are the number of women in some occupations not traditionally considered as female domains; actuaries and economists are examples. Does this indicate that in some fields of the workforce such as insurance and finance, prejudices against the employment of women are lessening? Are women themselves gaining more self-confidence in the contributions they can make in these areas?

Any previously held opinion that the majority of female mathematics graduates enter teaching is dispelled by the results of this table. Rather it is pleasing to note that women are entering a wide variety of occupations although the range of these is not yet as extensive as those of their male counterparts.

Table 13.5 is an extension of Table 13.4 in which the total number of graduates in each occupational group have been separated into three periods, two of four years and the last of three years, whilst the occupational groups have been put into ten broad categories. Category 'Other' comprises clerical, creative and arts, and miscellaneous. Percentages only have been used. These divisions and groupings have been designed not only to draw attention to the major distributional patterns of the occupations but also to any significant changes over the last 14 years.

One obvious movement is the decrease of both males and females entering teaching (educationalists). This loss is balanced by the numbers entering finance, commerce and insurance occupations.

The broad categorization of occupations into ten groupings indicates an overall

Table 13.5. *Percentage distribution over broad occupational categories of all employed mathematics graduates.*

Broad category of occupation	Percentage of employed mathematics graduates					
	1972/73–1976/77		1977/78–1981/82		1982/83–1985/86	
	M	F	M	F	M	F
Armed services personnel	2	0	3	0	3	0
Computing	18	17	22	21	16	10
Educationalists	45	40	27	27	25	29
Engineers	5	0	1	1	3	1
Finance, commerce	4	8	8	6	11	10
Insurance	8	6	14	6	15	15
Statisticians	5	13	9	21	7	13
Management	2	6	3	8	6	7
Scientists	7	6	9	6	9	9
Others	4	4	4	4	5	6
Total	100	100	100	100	100	100

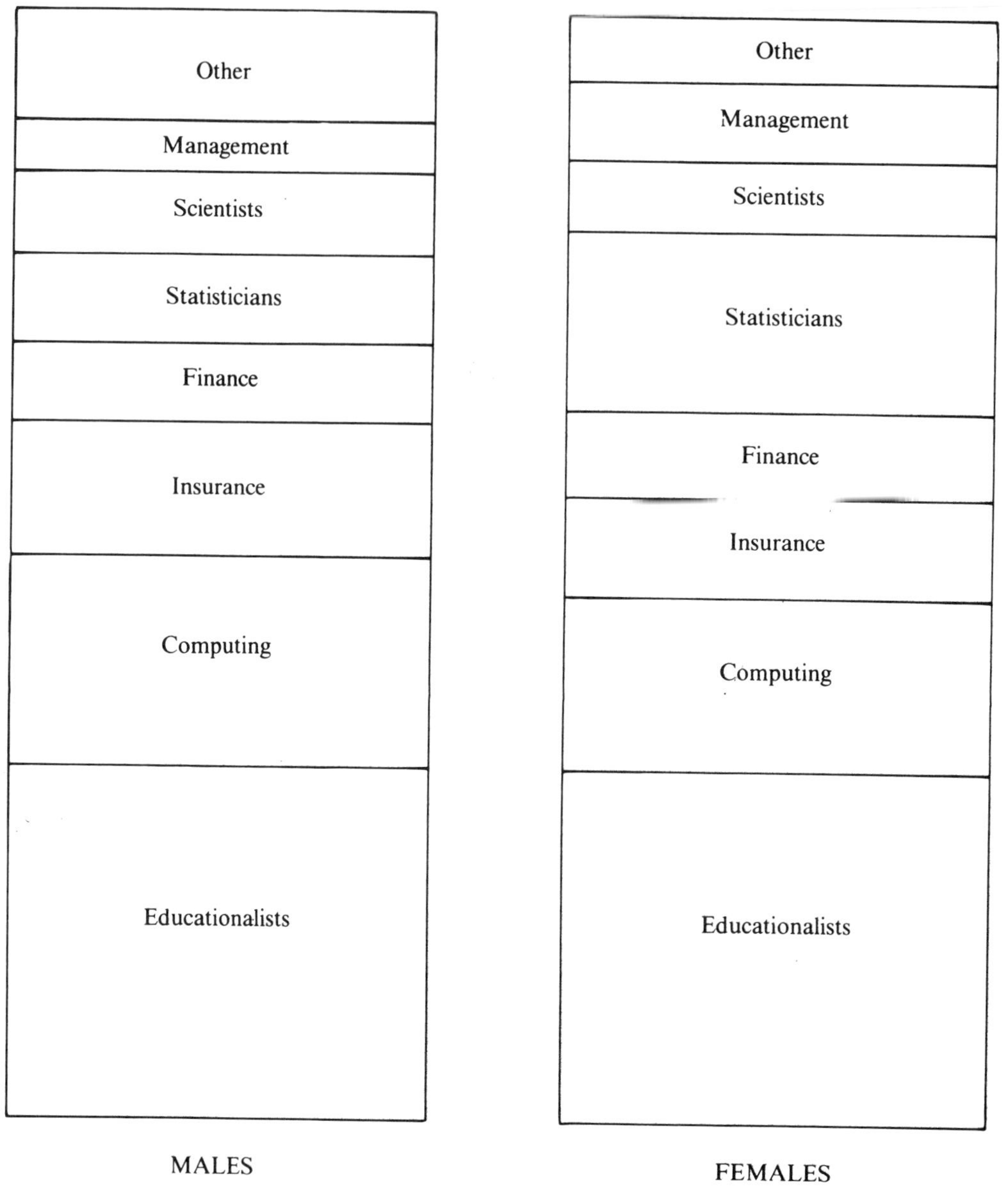

Figure 13.4   *A comparison of occupations by gender.*

similarity between the type of work of each sex. Figure 13.4 highlights this by using the totals over the full 14-year period. It is of note that, for both sexes, approximately 50 per cent of the occupations are computer or education linked.

WHERE ARE THE FUTURE MATHEMATICS TEACHERS?

Table 13.6 shows the number of mathematics graduates training for or practising school teaching.

Table 13.6. *Number of mathematics graduates training for or practising school teaching.*

Years	Primary teaching				Secondary teaching				Totals	
	Studying		Practising		Studying		Practising		Primary	Secondary
	M	F	M	F	M	F	M	F		
1972/73	4	4	1	2	22	12	24	10	11	58
1973/74	2	1	0	2	28	24	11	7	5	70
1974/75	2	2	0	0	20	20	15	8	4	63
1975/76	2	3	1	1	25	16	17	5	7	73
1976/77	0	2	0	3	30	19	15	2	5	66
1977/78	1	3	0	0	20	15	9	7	4	51
1978/79	1	0	1	0	27	19	8	5	2	59
1979/80	1	1	0	1	24	16	10	5	3	55
1980/81	0	1	0	0	11	17	14	3	1	45
1981/82	0	1	1	0	14	17	10	5	2	46
1982/83	0	0	1	0	7	13	10	8	1	38
1983/84	0	0	0	0	13	13	5	2	0	33
1984/85	0	0	1	0	14	13	11	8	1	46
1985/86	0	0	1	0	9	5	6	7	1	27

The declining number of mathematics graduates involved in school teaching is obvious. If the current trend continues, there will soon be no mathematics graduates entering the primary service and only a handful in the secondary service.

When it is considered that mathematics is a subject studied by all primary school and nearly all secondary school students, it gives cause for alarm that there will be no mathematics graduates to teach them in most schools. In any discipline, it is necessary to have teachers who are themselves graduates in their subject area. Their knowledge and confidence in their subject provides leadership among other teachers. At the senior level of secondary schooling, they convey this confidence to students who themselves become confident in the subject. If students are not getting adequate teaching in mathematics, they will not continue their studies in this discipline and the number of mathematics graduates will decrease further, producing a vicious circle.

Urgent consideration must be given to making school teaching more attractive to mathematics graduates.

CONCLUSIONS

The number of mathematics graduates is declining.

There is a slight increase in the number of women graduating in mathematics.

On average, forty per cent of mathematics graduates continue in further study while a third are in the workforce within six months of graduation.

Very few women advance to higher degrees.

Both male and female mathematics graduates enter a wide range of occupations, many of them with a statistical and analytical orientation, with the main employers being in the areas of education, computer services, statistics and insurance.

The supply of mathematics graduates entering teaching is decreasing alarmingly.

UPDATE

Prior to publication of this chapter, an update was completed on the statistics for the 1986/87 and 1987/88 years, the results of which, summarized, show that:

1. The trend of a decreasing number of mathematics graduates appears to be continuing. This is slightly more so for men, hence the resulting increase in the percentage of graduates who are women. In 1987/88, 35 per cent of mathematics graduates were female and this equalled the previous high in 1981/82.
2. The proportion of mathematics graduates entering employment in New Zealand within six months of graduating has been increasing to approximately 40 per cent of both male and female graduates in 1987/88. There has been a corresponding slight decrease in the proportion of mathematics graduates continuing full-time study. It will be interesting to see if this shift towards entering the workforce instead of further study continues in the next few years.
3. On average, 18 per cent of mathematics graduates were continuing in full-time study towards another degree, a similar proportion to the immediately previous years.
4. The range of occupations entered by mathematics graduates over these two years did not show any decrease in breadth. The distribution over the broad occupational categories for females was similar to the 1972/73–1985/86 period. However, for males, there were increases of 11 per cent in the proportion entering insurance and 6 per cent entering computing. This means that in the 1986/87–1987/88 period, almost half the male mathematics graduates entered insurance or computing mainly at the expense of education where the proportion decreased by 14 per cent.
5. The decrease in the number of mathematics graduates entering teaching appears to be continuing. As these numbers dwindle, intervention programmes to attract mathematics graduates to teaching become even more urgent.

It is hoped that this report will raise an awareness of the present situation regarding mathematics graduates in New Zealand. Some areas of concern have been identified of which the most serious are the decreasing supply of mathematics graduates, the disproportionately lower number of female graduates continuing to higher degrees and also the decrease in recent years in numbers entering teaching.

The causes of this situation have not been addressed nor have suggestions been made as to steps which might remedy the situation but a basis has been provided for further investigations. The necessity of mathematics in so much of our modern living must never be underestimated. It is essential that all areas including education, research, finance and industry be served by highly qualified mathematicians. Progress is dependent upon their knowledge and expertise.

ACKNOWLEDGEMENT

We are grateful to Mr F. Whiteling, Graduate Appointments Officer, and to Mr P.B. Henry, systems analyst, at Canterbury University, New Zealand, for their interest, helpfulness and the provision of the data used in this report.

Chapter 14

Women and Mathematical Research in Italy During the Period 1887–1946

Giuseppina Fenaroli, Fulvia Furinghetti, Antonio Garibaldi and Anna Somaglia

This chapter is the result of research carried out on the Italian scientific journals of the period 1887–1946 in order to provide a file of women's mathematical papers and some related statistical figures.

It seems to us that this work may constitute a first step in the direction suggested in 1897 by Gustaf Eneström, whose answer to the question 'à quel degré la femme est-elle capable de science?' was '. . . pour répondre définitivement à cette question, il faut en premier lieu une analyse détaillée et impartiale des travaux scientifiques des femmes, et cette analyse nous manque encore, . . .' (Eneström, 1897, p. 25).

BACKGROUND

The observation that progress in mathematical research is especially due to males is one of the classical elements in support of the 'female inferiority' thesis in mathematics, and, in the literature of mathematics education, the number of papers still considering the problem of sex difference in mathematical performances (Fox, 1980; Burton and Townsend, 1985; Fennema, 1985) provides further evidence that the question is still under discussion.

The papers of some authors (see, for example, Clements, 1979; Perl, 1979; Kroll, 1985) show that an historical approach may enrich this discussion with further useful elements. We agree with this point of view. Our contribution concerns female scientific production in mathematics in Italy during the period from 1887 (the year in which for the first time a woman graduated in mathematics in the new unified state of Italy) until 1946 (the beginning of the second post-war period).

In order to give a global frame to our work we divided the history of female presence in scientific and, particularly, mathematical research into three main periods.

1. The pioneering period: from early European history until the first half of the nineteenth century.
2. The period of taking up of awareness: from the second half of the nineteenth century to the second world war.
3. The present period: from World War II until today.

In the first period, that may be considered as the prehistory of female presence in mathematics, the number of women doing mathematical research was very scant. Nevertheless some women achieved distinction in mathematics (Tee, 1983), for instance:

- Hypatia (375–415), daughter of Theon, the well-known editor and scholiast of Euclidean works; she lived in Alexandria
- Émilie du Châtelet (France, 1706–1749); she was connected with Maupertuis, Voltaire and Clairaut
- Maria Gaetana Agnesi (Italy, 1718–1799), of a noble rich family
- Sophie Germain (France, 1776–1831); she was connected with Gauss
- Ada Byron, Countess of Lovelace (Great Britain, 1815–1852), daughter of the poet Lord Byron
- Mary Somerville (Great Britain, 1780–1872), daughter of a Scottish Admiral
- and others, especially astronomers

All these women mathematicians have to be considered as exceptional and isolated cases in their social and cultural environments. They are not the effect of a specific educational policy, but the effect of certain circumstances: an extraordinary brain, of course, but also a 'distinguished' social position or a relationship (such as sisters, daughters) with male scientists.

The third period, on the contrary, seems to offer women of developed countries opportunities comparable with those of men. For example, in Italy, during the year 1985, the percentages of graduate women (of all graduates in the same solar year) were as follows (Istituto Centrale di Statistica, 1986):

Mathematics	75.0%	(962 graduate women out of 1284 graduates)
Scientific group	59.5%	(mathematics included)
Medical group	34.3%	
Engineering and architecture	16.9%	
Agrarian group	25.6%	
Economics	30.8%	
Political and Social Sciences	40.4%	
Law	44.5%	
Humanistic and Philosophical group	79.6%	

The high percentages favourable to women are not preserved in their post-degree careers (see for instance Rothschild, 1983, 1986). Table 14.1 (from the Annuari del CNR) provides interesting food for thought.

The second period is very interesting and crucial in the history of women mathematicians. It presents important changes concerning the diffusion of the culture among women and the increase of female presence in some intellectual activities which until that time were quite devoid of women's contribution (Benetti-Brunelli, 1932).

As far as Italy is concerned, we meet Ernestina Paper as the first woman who took a degree (in 1877 at 'Istituto di Studi Superiori' of Firenze, in medicine). We use the word 'degree' to indicate the different kinds of certificates it has been possible to take in Italian universities or analogous institutes after the diploma in high school (Cuyper, 1879). (Here we do not discuss the Italian system of education, which is described

Table 14.1. *Directors of Institutes and Centres of National Research Council in Italy in 1984.*

Subjects	Males	Females
Mathematics	7	–
Physics	30	–
Chemistry	53	2
Biology and Medicine	37	4
Geology	24	1
Agriculture	40	1
Engineering and Architecture	25	1
History, Philosophy, Philology	13	1
Law and Political Sciences	3	–
Economy, Social Science, Statistics	5	–
Technological research	21	–
Total	258	10

in Unione Matematica Italiana, 1988.) From statistical sources (Istituto Centrale di Statistica, 1976; Ravà, 1902) we obtain the following trend per decades of percentages of degrees conferred on women compared with the total number of degrees from 1881 to 1950. As the first woman graduated in 1877, we start from that decade 1881–90 (until 1880 only three women graduated):

1881–1890	0.7%	(21/2912)
1891–1900	6%	(233/3681)
1901–1910	5%	(211/3951)
1911–1920	8%	(368/4622)
1921–1930	14%	(1166/8279)
1931–1940	17%	(2020/11628)
1941–1950	28%	(5115/18479)

The figures represent the number of degrees obtained by women compared with the total number of degrees. It is impossible to find out how many obtained more that one degree. We know that in the first decade 20 women graduated and 201 in the second one. Therefore some women obtained more than one degree (we know one obtained three degrees). We observe that this problem is less relevant when the figures increase in the successive periods.

The data above give evidence of the important changes in the evolution of female cultural presence in Italy, between the last decades of the nineteenth century and the beginning of the twentieth century. Italy became a unified state in 1861. The new state inherited different systems of education, different cultures and different policies from its constituent parts and, moreover, a problem of illiteracy. In this situation women had few opportunities to work, salaries lower than those of men, responsibility for children, no vote, fewer opportunities than men for attending school, even at low levels. The situation evolved significantly in the last decades of the nineteenth century: this evolution is linked with female movements all over the world and active also in Italy. A literature exists (for instance Pieroni-Bortolotti, 1963) which gives information on women's education and analyses the phenomenon of women's emancipation with its social, political, cultural and affective connections.

Among all the aspects of women's emancipation, the professional opportunities for teaching are important. Indeed, having increased their intellectual culture women realized that the profession of teacher was a good route for their evolution in society. At that time (after 1861) women as teachers had been accepted in pre-university schools in Italy, especially in primary schools (a degree was not required for being a teacher in primary school). From the last decade of the nineteenth century, the number of women teaching in primary school increased more and more. At the beginning of the twentieth century a journal for women teachers in primary school (*Il Corriere delle maestre*) already existed (Ravà, 1902).

We think that the main causes of this increase may be that, generally speaking, in Italy teaching is considered a profession requiring 'human' qualities usually ascribed to women and on the social ladder teachers are not considered important (this, in particular, means low salaries, and teaching may be considered a part-time job).

So our hypothesis is that women grasped one of their first opportunities of emancipation by choosing to enter a profession seen to be more congenial to their nature and less desired by men. In addition, we think that this fact influenced university curricula of women because the degrees seen as being more suitable for being appointed teacher to secondary school are those in humanities, mathematics, natural sciences, physics. These degrees became more and more popular with women.

HISTORICAL SOURCES AND METHODOLOGY

We have concentrated on the second period in investigating women graduates in mathematics and their scientific production in mathematics. Last year we had the opportunity of studying the rich historical material (Fenaroli *et al.*, 1988) which is in the Library of the Department of Mathematics (University of Genova). This research focused and supported our interest. Indeed this chapter stems from the presence in this library of a collection of about 14,500 articles, in separate printing, and booklets that from now on we will call the 'Loria Collection'.

This important mathematical material belonged to Gino Loria (1862–1954), full professor of Geometria Superiore at the Institute of Mathematics of University of Genova for almost 50 years (until 1935) and also known for his studies on the history of mathematics. The 'Loria Collection' mainly concerns the period we are considering. It consists of papers Loria received either as a gift (he was on many editorial boards of journals) or acquired through his studies. The material of the 'Loria Collection' was a starting point for our work, but the way Loria acquired this material could not guarantee a satisfactory sample of mathematical production in the period we are considering (Fenaroli *et al.*, 1988). So, to improve our data, we decided to look at all papers by women published in Italy in important mathematical journals and proceedings in the period at issue (Pirillo, 1977).

In Italy the great tradition of academies and universities provided a good cultural background for the new unified state: mathematical research was quite advanced in comparison with the international community (S.I.P.S., 1939; Tricomi, 1962; Bottazzini, 1981; Gambini and Pepe, 1983; Albers *et al.*, 1987; Guerraggio, 1987). A number of scientific journals were published in Italy: the articles were mainly written in Italian, some in French or German, a few in English. Moreover, the journals published some translations of foreign material. Most of the journals were linked with universities and academies and the editorial boards mainly consisted of university professors and it seems that Italian mathematicians published predominantly in Italian journals.

We consulted the journals listed in Table 14.2. To catalogue every paper written by a woman we used the following categories:

- Author of the paper
- Date and place of the writing out
- Title of the paper
- Bibliography (yes–no)
- Journal
- Publishing date
- Review of the paper (if available and relevant)
- Other notes about the author (university of the degree, supervising professor, information about career after the degree, etc.).

EVIDENCE ON WOMEN IN MATHEMATICS FROM THE 'LORIA COLLECTION'

Reviewing the 'Loria Collection' provoked a lot of emotions because so many and so various are the memories it contains about a recent slot of our history. The collection contained: 66 Italian women authors, 423 Italian men authors. The 175 papers by women are distributed as follows:

1 from 1887 to 1899
38 from 1900 to 1919
136 from 1920 to 1946

The earliest paper in the Collection by a woman, was published in 1895 in *Giornale di Matematiche di Battaglini*. It was by Lia Predella, who took her degree at the University of Pavia in 1894 and concerned differential equations. The distribution of the 66 women authors in the Collection is as follows:

45 with 1 paper each
12 with 2 or 3 papers each
 4 with 4 or 5 papers each
 2 with 7 papers each
 1 with 9 papers
 2 with more than 9 papers each

In Italy, in order to have a degree conferred it is necessary to write a dissertation, which is published if it is considered relevant. Thus many of these papers concern the subject of the author's dissertation. The two women authors with more than 9 papers are Margherita Beloch (married Piazzolla) (see Gambini and Pepe, 1983) and Maria Pastori (see Udeschini, 1976), who worked, respectively, in geometry and mathematical physics.

We found six papers in the 'Loria Collection', all except the most recent written by males, specifically treating the subject Women and Mathematics. They are outlined below.

Table 14.2. *Italian mathematical journals and proceedings used in the study.*

Abbreviation	Title of the journal	Place of issue	First year of printing
AIV	ATTI DEL (REALE) ISTITUTO VENETO DI SCIENZE LETTERE ED ARTI	Venezia	1840
AMPA	ANNALI DI MATEMATICA PURA ED APPLICATA formerly ANNALI DI SCIENZE MATEMATICHE E FISICHE	Roma, at first	1850
GB	GIORNALE DI MATEMATICHE DI BATTAGLINI originally GIORNALE DI MATEMATICHE AD USO DEGLI STUDENTI DELLE UNIVERSITÀ ITALIANE PUBBLICATO PER CURA DEL PROF. G. BATTAGLINI	Napoli	1863
ILR	(REALE) ISTITUTO LOMBARDO DI SCIENZE E LETTERE-RENDICONTI	Milano	1864
ATo	ATTI DELLA (REALE) ACCADEMIA DI SCIENZE DI TORINO	Torino	1865
APi	ANNALI DELLA (REGIA) SCUOLA NORMALE SUPERIORE DI PISA – CLASSE DI SCIENZE (FISICHE E MATEMATICHE)	Pisa	1871
CPa	RENDICONTI DEL CIRCOLO MATEMATICO DI PALERMO	Palermo	1884
AL	ATTI DELLA (REALE) ACCADEMIA DEI LINCEI For this journal we considered only the part called RENDICONTI, started in 1885, excluding the part called MEMORIE. From 1939 until 1944 the ACCADEMIA DEI LINCEI was absorbed by the ACCADEMIA D'ITALIA, whose RENDICONTI have been consulted. The ATTI DELLA ACCADEMIA PONTIFICIA DEI NUOVI LINCEI, started in 1847, have not been considered	Roma	1885
AGe	ATTI DELL'ACCADEMIA LIGURE DI SCIENZE E LETTERE originally ATTI DELLA SOCIETÀ DI SCIENZE E LETTERE DI GENOVA	Genova	1890
RMRo	RENDICONTI DI MATEMATICA (UNIVERSITÀ DEGLI STUDI DI ROMA E ISTITUTO NAZIONALE DI ALTA MATEMATICA) formerly RENDICONTI DEL SEMINARIO MATEMATICO DELLA FACOLTÀ DI SCIENZE DELL' UNIVERSITÀ DI ROMA	Roma	1913
BUMI	BOLLETTINO DELLA UNIONE MATEMATICA ITALIANA	Bologna	1922
SeMi	RENDICONTI DEL SEMINARIO MATEMATICO E FISICO DI MILANO	Milano	1927
SePa	RENDICONTI DEL SEMINARIO MATEMATICO DELLA (REGIA) UNIVERSITÀ DI PADOVA	Padova	1930
SeTo	RENDICONTI DEL SEMINARIO MATEMATICO DELL' UNIVERSITÀ E POLITECNICO DI TORINO formerly CONFERENZE DI FISICA E MATEMATICA	Torino	1931

1. 'Les femmes dans la science' by the historian of mathematics A. Rebière (1894)

In this booklet of 88 pages, the author describes in detail the life and the work of Hypatia, Émilie du Châtelet, Maria Gaetana Agnesi, Sophie Germain, Mary Somerville and Sofya Kowalevsky. At the end of the book Rebière explains his point of view about the kinds of women interested in scientific studies:

> Pour préciser l'influence—plus réelle qu'on ne croit—des femmes sur les progrès des sciences, il faudrait étudier, d'abord et surtout, les *savantes professionnelles*, celles qui ont consacré aux études scientifiques la plus grande partie de leur vie: philosophes, mathématiciennes, physiciennes et naturalistes.
>
> On passerait aussi en revue le *simples curieuses*, qui, livrées à d'autres travaux, ont touché pourtant aux sciences proprement dites. Ainsi Madame de Staël a de belles pages sur la philosophie des sciences; George Sand était passionnée pour la botanique et la minéralogie.
>
> Viendraient ensuite les *collaboratrices*, qui ont aidé les savants, activement et discrètement . . . Il ne faudrait pas oublier enfin les *protectrices*, qui ont fondé des prix dans les académies ou répandu leurs bienfaits sous d'autres formes.
>
> (pp. 79–80)

The second edition of this book (Rebière, 1897) contains a wider list (about 600) of 'Scientist women' and is enhanced by biographical notes.

In the same period an analogous work on women in sciences appeared (Valentin, 1895).

2. 'Le laureate in Italia' by Vittore Ravà, (1902)

In this work the author, a university professor, likes to notice that *the female movement has gone ahead very quickly*, and that

> la donna italiana tende alla conquista di una migliore condizione giuridica e sociale per la via più sicura, accrescendo cioè la propria cultura intellettuale.
>
> Essa non frequenta più la sola scuola normale per divenire maestra elementare; ma accorre ad ogni ordine di scuole secondarie, sia classiche, sia tecniche, sia professionali; né s'arresta alle porte dell'Università, ché anzi percorre con pieno successo, anche gli studi superiori di ogni genere.
>
> (p. 4)

He supports his opinion by some statistical figures, for example:

- In 1900 the girls studying in licei and technical schools were 5513 while they were a few tens about 20 years before.
- Until 1889 there were very few graduate females in Italy; in 1893 the number of girls studying at university was 98 and in 1900 this number increased to more than 250.

He also gives a detailed list of women graduating in Italy from 1861 to 1900, specifying the university, the year and the kind of degree. From the collected data he draws up a table reporting the number of degrees assigned to women in Italy, classified by university and by faculty and another table with analogous data by year and by faculty. We summarize these data as follows:

1. first year a woman graduated: 1877
2. first year a woman graduated in Mathematics: 1887
3. total number of graduate women: 224
   in Humanities: 177
   in Sciences: 30
   in Medicine: 24
   in Mathematics: 20
   in Law: 6

Ravà reports the names of the graduate women. Among them are Anna Kulishoff (Medicine), Giulia Sofia Bakunin (Medicine), Marussia Bakunin (Chemistry), and the famous pedagogue Maria Montessori (Medicine). (For a discussion of the difficulties of access for women to Italian universities in the first years of unified Italy see Pieroni-Bortolotti, 1963).

3. 'Donne Matematiche' by Gino Loria (1936)

In this article the author, as historian of mathematics, describes some principal women mathematicians, partially inspired by the books of Rebière. But, while Rebière concludes confidently that the future of women as mathematicians will be glorious, Loria concludes the opposite, that is that women have no possibilities in mathematical research. In favour of women he only recognizes that the task of women of our times is much higher than that assigned in the Roman age, of keeping house and spinning wool. Moreover, he reports with indignation the project of law aiming at forbidding women to learn reading and writing of Sylvain Maréchal in the eighteenth century (Rebière, 1897), and the 'Society of women haters' against women in university (he quotes the journal *Minerva*, 1901).

To support his thesis on women's attitudes towards mathematics in a note, he quotes two significant sentences: (i) Lombroso (the famous criminologist) and Ferrero in the book *La donna delinquente, la prostituta e la donna normale* (The criminal, prostitute and normal woman) (Roux, Torino-Roma, 1893, p. 548) wrote that Nicarete (called by Loria a substantially unknown person) did not deny her favours to anybody who would teach something to her [in geometry]; (ii) P.G. Möbius (nephew of the famous mathematician) in his *Ueber die Anlage zur Mathematik* (J.P.A. Barth, Leipzig, 1900, p. 85), wrote 'Then we can tell that woman mathematician is against nature, in some sense she is an hermaphrodite'.

Loria's attitude seems very ambiguous, but more unfavourable to women in comparison with that expressed 50 years after by another famous Italian geometer, Francesco Severi (1951).

4. 'La donna nella matematica' by Umberto Ceretti (1902)

This author is more drastic than Gino Loria about women's inferiority in mathematics. Starting from his experience as teacher and researcher in the history of mathematics, he strengthens Loria's conclusions by observing that women, even if they take a degree, only reach good positions in their profession with difficulty. Then he cites the favourable opinions about women working in mathematics of some important people (Poullain, Edgworth, Riballier, Glardon, Dupuy, Lafitte, Mellier, and Klein, the famous mathematician), convinced supporters of women scientists, but he also cites the diametrically opposed opinions of other authors (Fontenelle, Kant, Lamennais, De Candolle, Lombroso, De Goncourt, Loiseau, Voltaire, De Girardin, Charaux, Marion e Legouvé), all of whom believed that women have few abilities to be good researchers.

5. 'La riforma della scuole medie e l'istruzione della donna' by the high school teacher Giulio Fasella (1906)

This article is an interesting contribution to the debate on secondary education of women. The author assumes that some jobs (he does not report professions) are reserved for women and so women need special schools. He is against co-education because of differences in character (not skills), but he recognizes that it is possible to obtain good results when teaching girls, in using particular techniques of education. The author does not describe these techniques. Analogous arguments on co-education and mathematics for boys and girls were developed in the plenary lecture of David Eugene Smith in the I.C.M. of Rome (1908).

6. 'Responsabilità dell'insegnante nella formazione morale dell'alunno' by Maria Giovanna Sittignani (1944)

This more recent article is written by a woman who was an appreciated teacher of mathematics in high school and author of some scientific papers. It is a booklet of instructions for being a good teacher: the problem of co-education is considered only from the point of view of the problems of behaviour and of the difference in character of the pupils, while there are no worries about sex differences in mathematical performance: as the author is a mathematics teacher, her opinion is important and significant on this point. It is remarkable that the author thinks it may be a problem to be a female teacher of male pupils. The contrary (a male teacher with female pupils) seems to the author less problematic.

EVIDENCE FROM ITALIAN JOURNALS

We know that our research is not exhaustive but we are convinced that the figures given and, in particular, the percentages given are very significant. On the other hand, already at the time of Rebière, in the review of the second edition of his book (Rebière, 1897), Gustaf Eneström writes, 'Il va sans dire qu'un ouvrage tel que celui dont nous nous occupons, ne saurait jamais devenir ni complet ni tout à fait exact' (Eneström, 1897, p. 25).

We have investigated the number of people engaged in mathematical research, finding in total 1170 people; 234 are women and 936 men, 20 per cent of women distributed over the three periods as follows:

	Women	Men	Total	% women
1887–1899	4	267	271	1.5
1900–1919	75	383	458	16.4
1920–1946	158	544	702	22.5

We repeat that we considered in our research graduate women only. If all women writing mathematical papers are considered the figures are not substantially changed, except perhaps in the first period.

When considering the number of articles in journals the results are quite different: women contributed 546 articles compared to 8182 articles by men. Women's articles represent only 6.2 per cent of the whole number.

In order to enrich our analysis we also considered the communications presented by Italian women to Int. Math. Congresses (from 1897 to 1936) and to the Congresses of Unione Matematica Italiana (Italian Mathematical Association) held in 1937 and 1940; no Italian women gave plenary lectures in this period. The first woman to give a plenary lecture at I.C.M. was Emmy Noether in 1932.

Table 14.3 gives figures and percentages referring to every journal examined (see Table 14.2).

Comparing those authors who published five or more papers with those who published less than five, we found the following:

	≥ 5 papers	< 5 papers
women	20	214
men	313	623

We notice that 8.5 per cent of women and 33.4 per cent of men wrote five or more papers and conclude that more women than men limited their engagement in research. This appears to be the case because of marriage and responsibility for childcare. Of course,

Table 14.3.

Abbreviation	Number of women's articles	Number of men's articles	Total number of articles	% women's articles versus total number of articles in journals
AIV	32	425	457	7
AMPA	13	615	628	2
GB	84	813	897	9.4
IRL	77	786	863	8.9
ATo	46	659	705	6.5
APi	7	185	192	3.6
CPa	72	839	911	7.9
AL	144	2730	2874	5
AGe	3	48	51	5.9
RMRo	11	195	206	5.3
BUMI	43	653	696	6.2
SeMi	6	101	107	5.6
SePa	7	105	112	6.2
SeTo	1	28	29	3.4
Total	546	8182	8728	6.2

Communications	Number of women's communications	Number of men's communications	Total number of communications	% Women's communications versus total number of communications
Int. Math. Congresses	8	145	153	5.2
UMI Congresses	8	128	136	5.9

both men and women stop scientific production because of difficulties with university career advancement and the links to supervision of research. Two anecdotes demonstrate this. In a scientific report (S.I.P.S., 1939), Enea Bortolotti observes that the geometrical school of Giuseppe Vitali stopped at his death and refers explicitly in a note to the papers of two women who worked in this field. Secondly, we found two women in Genoa who, before 1917, published papers in the field of partial differential equations inspired by Eugenio Elia Levi. Unfortunately, he died in 1917 during the first world war and the scientific effort of his pupils ceased.

From the list by Ravà (1902), we know that the first graduate woman in mathematics was Iginia Massarini in 1887 at the University of Napoli. She translated and annotated Tchebicheff's book on the theory of congruences (Frattini, 1895; Massarini, 1895). From 1887 to 1899, 19 women got mathematical degrees and at least 4 of them wrote scientific papers: Emma Bortolotti, Cornelia Fabri, Iginia Massarini and Lia Predella.

In spite of this good beginning in the last decade of the nineteenth century and the favourable trend in the first two decades of the twentieth century, it was not until 1921 that a woman was appointed full professor in Mathematics at an Italian university. She was Pia Nalli who got a chair of Analysis at the University of Cagliari (Fichera, 1965).

Among the women who published papers in the period 1887–1946 six reached full professorship. They were: Pia Nalli (Analysis), Margherita Beloch (married Piazzolla) (Geometry), Maria Pastori (Mathematical Physics), Maria Cibrario (married Cinquini) (Analysis), Giuseppina Biggioggero (married Masotti) (Geometry), Cesarina Tibiletti (married Marchionna) (Geometry).

ACKNOWLEDGEMENTS

The authors wish to thank Professors Paolo Boero, Jaures P. Cecconi and Luigi Pepe for their help during the development of the research.

REFERENCES

Albers, D. J., Alexanderson, G. L. and Reid, C. (1987) *International Mathematical Congresses. An Illustrated History 1893–1986.* New York: Springer-Verlag.
Benetti-Brunelli, V. (1932) 'Donne'. *Enciclopedia Italiana di Scienze, Lettere ed Arti.* Milano: Edizioni Istituto G. Treccani, pp. 146–152.
Bottazzini, U. (1981) Mathematics in a Unified Italy. In Mehertens, H., Bos, H. and Schneider, I. (eds) *Social History of Nineteenth Century Mathematics.* Boston: Birkhäuser, pp. 165–178.
Burton, L. and Townsend, R. (1985) Girl-friendly mathematics. *Mathematics Teaching*, **111**, 2–6.
Ceretti, U. (1902) La donna nella matematica. *Rivista di Fisica, Matematica e Scienze Naturali*, **10** (31), 627–634.
Clements, (Ken) M. A. (1979) Sex differences in mathematical performances: an historical perspective. *Educational Studies in Mathematics*, **10** (3), 306–322.

Cuyper, A. C. (De) (1879) *Les Universités Royales en Italie*. Liège: Imprimerie de J. Desver.

Eneström, G. (1897) A. Rebière les femmes dans le science [Recensionen]. *Bibliotheca Mathematica* (neue folge), **11** (1), 25–27.

Fasella, G. (1906) *La riforma delle scuole medie e l'istuizione della donna*. Milano: Vallardi.

Fenaroli, G., Furinghetti, F., Garibaldi, A.C. and Somaglia, A.M. (1988) Collezioni speciali esistenti nella biblioteca matematica dell' Università di Genova, Atti del Convegno *Pietro Riccardi e la storiografia delle matematiche in italia*. Bologna: Pitagora, pp. 219–230.

Fennema, E. (ed) (1985) Explaining sex-related differences in Mathematics: theoretical models. *Educational Studies in Mathematics*, **16**(3), 303–320.

Fichera, G. (1965) Pia Nalli *B. U. M. I.* (serie 3), **20** (4), 544–549.

Fox, L. (1980) *The Problem of Women and Mathematics*. New York: Ford Foundation.

Frattini, G. (1895) Notizia della traduzione italiana del libro-Tchebicheff (P.L.): Teoria delle congruenze, *Periodico di Matematica*, **10**, 193.

Gambini, G. and Pepe, L. (1983) La raccolta Montesano di opusculi nella bibliotecea dell' Istituto Matematico dell' Università di Ferrara. *Internal Report*, Istituto di Matematica, Università di Ferrara.

Guerraggio, A. (ed.) (1987) *La matematica italiana tra le due guerre mondiali*. Bologna: Pitagora.

Istituto Centrale di Statistica (1976) *Sommario di statistiche storiche d' Italia: 1861-1975*. Roma: Tip. Failli.

Istituto Centrale di Statistica (1986) *Annuario statistico dell' istruzione*, Vol. 37. Calliano (Tn): Manfrini R. Arti grafiche Vallegemma.

Kroll, D. (1985) Evidence from the *Mathematics Teacher* (1908-1920) on women and mathematics. *For the Learning of Mathematics*, **5** (2), 7–10.

Loria, G. (1936) Donne Matematiche, in Scritti, conferenze e discorsi sulla storia delle matematiche, CEDAM, Padova, pp. 447–466. (The text of a conference held in 1901 in Mantua and published in *Atti Regia Accademia Virgiliana di Mantova*, in 1902. The author writes at the beginning of the article that a French translation exists in the *Revue Scientifique* (1904).)

Massarini, I. (1895) *Teoria delle congruenze di P.L. Tchebicheff, traduzione italiana con aggiunte e note*. Roma: E. Loescher.

Perl, T. (1979) The ladies' diary or women's almanack, 1704-1841, *Historia Mathematica*, **6** (1), 36–53.

Pieroni-Bortolotti, F. (1963) *Alle origini del movimento femminile in Italia 1848-1892*. Torino: Einaudi.

Pirillo, G. (1977) Indagine bibliografica sulle pubblicazioni matematiche periodiche italiane, *N. U. M. I.*, **4** (11), 18–37.

Ravà, V. (1902) *Le laureate in Italia. Notizie statistiche*. Roma: Cecchini.

Rebière, A. (1894) *Les Femmes dans la Science*. Paris: Libraire Nony et C.

Rebière, A. (1897) *Les Femmes dans la Science*. Paris: Libraire Nony et C., II édition.

Rothschild, J. (ed.) (1983) *Machina ex Dea*. Oxford: Pergamon. (Trad. it. (1986), *Donne tecnologia scienza*. Introduzione all' edizione Italiana di E. Donini. Torino: Rosenberg e Sellier.)

Severi, F. (1951) La donna e la matematica, *Archimede*, **3**, 210–212.

S.I.P.S. (1939) *Un secolo di progresso scientifico italiano 1839-1939*, Vol. 1, Matematica. Milano: Hoepli.

Sittignani, M.G. (1944) *Responsabilità dell' insegnante nella formazione morale dell' alunno*. Roma: Studium, No. 9.

Tee, G.J. (1983) The pioneering women mathematicians, *The Mathematical Intelligencer*, **5** (4), 27–36.

Tricomi, F.G. (1962) Matematici italiani nel primo secolo dello stato unitario, *Memorie dell' Accademia delle Scienze di Torino, Classe Scienze Fisiche, Matematiche, Naturali* (serie 4), **1** (1), 1–20.

Udeschini, P. (1976) Maria Pastori. *Istituto Lombardo di Scienze e Lettere - Rendiconti, Parte Generale e Atti Ufficiali, Milano*, **110**, 92–98.

Unione Matematica Italiana (1988) *Mathematical Education in Italy*. Padova: Decibel editrice.

Valentin, G. (1895) Die Frauen in den exakten Wissenschaften. *Bibliotheca Mathematica*, (neue folge), **9** (3), 65–76.

Conclusion

Leone Burton

In one way or another all the chapters in the book sing a similar song whether their focus is on the past or the present, on classroom experience or attainment. The theme of that song is the complexity of the relationship between gender and mathematics education as well as the necessity of embedding research into the general sociopolitical context, even where one slice of mathematics learning experience is providing data on single variables. Thus, whether considering primary school pupils in Greece, secondary school pupils in Singapore, students in further education in Australia or faculty members teaching mathematics in the USA, all the authors have drawn attention to the effects of the social climate in construing and constraining choices and behaviour in mathematics. One important component of this is teacher behaviour, another personal and social expectations. Initially seen as a somewhat arbitrary and eclectic collection held together only by the common thread of gender, this volume can now be viewed as reinforcing a persistent plea in the mathematics education literature to respect the learner in her or his attempts to make sense of the new in the context of the old and to respect the discipline of mathematics *education* for those concerns which are distinctive from the content, that is, mathematics. The distinctive concerns of mathematics education address the psychology, sociology and anthropology of learning and teaching mathematics utilizing qualitative research methodologies which delve in depth into personal experience, as well as quantitative statistical techniques which paint a broad picture. Equal opportunities concerns highlight, again, how important is the voice of the person in enlightening and enlivening the general perspective. Small-scale studies help to point the way towards difficult questions or unaddressed issues which will become the focus of future research.

In constructing a research agenda, many such questions remain. At the international level, there is a need for a databank on performance, classroom strategies, pupil expectations, etc. There is a role for Unesco here but also researchers in richer countries could help their less financially fortunate colleagues by constructing and appealing for funding for cross-cultural studies. At the national level, many particular issues need systematic exploration. For example, what are the links between language and mathematics learning and how are these influenced by, for example, discussion, the negotiation of meaning, collaborative work? With a growing concern about assessment from the individual and the societal point of view, we need to know how pupils' attainment in mathematics, their attitudes towards the subject, and their ultimate social competency are affected by such different assessment strategies as profiling, records of achievement, continuous assessment, multichoice tests, staged examinations, open book examinations, group assessment, and so on. What effects are there on pupils' choices of disciplines and their attainment in gender-segregated settings? What helps to establish the gender/mathematics link in young children's minds? Can this be influenced and how?

When addressing curriculum development, some of the contributors in this volume have demonstrated the need to construct curricula which respond to the interests and experiences of all students. A resource bank of effective strategies, 'rich' materials which are gender-friendly, alternative forms of assessment would help to avoid the re-invention of the wheel. Mathematical topics need to be interrogated from an equal opportunities perspective using an approach such as that recorded in this volume by Mary Barnes and Mary Coupland, and the results of that interrogation made widely available. At the same time, the role of mathematics across other disciplines needs to be exploited so that fragmentation of learning is overcome and mathematics is encountered in contexts that are meaningful to the learner.

Finally, because of the interlocking between personal, social, curriculum and pedagogical influences, as researchers and curriculum developers we have a responsibility also to support the development of an action agenda. This would identify and publicize the many intervention strategies already in use, and invent new ones to influence the cultural and educational climate. Where research results are well-substantiated, policy makers need to be made aware of these and publicity sought to raise public awareness of the learning outcomes of continuing certain practices.

Ensuring that societies can be enriched by the mathematical contributions of their citizens and that individuals can feel positive about themselves in relation to the learning and use of mathematics is very obviously neither a straightforward nor simple task. The challenge is there.

Name Index

Subject Index

Eddie Ryan
OfNo 1294 ||
£16·99

Death Attitudes and the Older Adult

The Series in Death, Dying, and Bereavement
Consulting Editor
Robert A. Neimeyer

Davies—*Shadows in the Sun: The Experiences of Sibling Bereavement in Childhood*
Klass—*The Spiritual Lives of Bereaved Parents*
Harvey—*Perspectives on Loss: A Sourcebook*
Leenaars—*Lives and Deaths: Selections from the Works of Edwin S. Shneidman*
Martin, Doka—*Men Don't Cry . . . Women Do: Transcending Gender Stereotypes of Grief*
Nord—*Mutiple AIDS-Related Loss: A Handbook for Understanding and Surviving a Perpetual Fall*
Tomer—*Death Attitudes and the Older Adult: Theories, Concepts, and Applications*
Werth—*Contemporary Perspectives on Rational Suicide*

FORMERLY THE **SERIES IN DEATH EDUCATION, AGING, AND HEALTH CARE**
HANNELORE WASS, CONSULTING EDITOR

Selected Titles
Benoliel—*Death Education for the Health Professional*
Bertman—*Facing Death: Images, Insights, and Interventions*
Brammer—*How to Cope with Life Transitions: The Challenge of Personal Change*
Cleiren—*Bereavement and Adaptation: A Comparative Study of the Aftermath of Death*
Connor—*Hospice: Practice, Pitfalls, and Promise*
Corless, Pittman-Lindeman—*AIDS: Principles, Practices, and Politics, Abridged Edition*
Corless, Pittman-Lindeman—*AIDS: Principles, Practices, and Politics, Reference Edition*
Davidson—*The Hospice: Development and Administration, Second Edition*
Davidson, Linnolla—*Risk Factors in Youth Suicide*
Degner, Beaton—*Life–Death Decisions in Health Care*
Doka—*AIDS, Fear and Society: Challenging the Dreaded Disease*
Doty—*Communication and Assertion Skills for Older Persons*
Epting, Neimeyer—*Personal Meanings of Death: Applications of Personal Construct Theory to Clinical Practice*
Haber—*Health Care for an Aging Society: Cost-Conscious Community Care and Self-Care Approaches*
Hughes—*Bereavement and Support: Healing in a Group Environment*
Irish, Lundquist, Nelsen—*Ethnic Variations in Dying, Death, and Grief: Diversity in Universality*
Klass, Silverman, Nickman—*Continuing Bonds: New Understandings of Grief*
Lair—*Counseling the Terminally Ill: Sharing the Journey*
Leenaars, Maltsberger, Neimeyer—*Treatment of Suicidal People*
Leenaars, Wenckstern—*Suicide Prevention in Schools*
Leng—*Psychological Care in Old Age*
Lindeman, Corby, Downing, Sanborn—*Alzheimer's Day Care: A Basic Guide*
Lund—*Older Bereaved Spouses: Research with Practical Applications*
Neimeyer—*Death Anxiety Handbook: Research, Instrumentation, and Application*
Nord—*Multiple AIDS-Related Loss: A Handbook for Understanding and Surviving a Perpetual Fall*
Papadatou, Papadatos—*Children and Death*
Ricker, Myers—*Retirement Counseling: A Practical Guide for Action*
Sherron, Lumsden—*Introduction to Educational Gerontology. Third Edition*
Stillion—*Death and Sexes: An Examination of Differential Longevity, Attitudes, Behaviors, and Coping Skills*
Stillion, McDowell, May—*Suicide Across the Life Span—Premature Exits*
Vachon—*Occupational Stress in the Care of the Critically Ill, the Dying, and the Bereaved*
Wass, Corr—*Childhood and Death*
Wass, Corr—*Helping Children Cope with Death: Guidelines and Resources. Second Edition*
Wass, Corr, Pacholski, Forfar—*Death Education II: An Annotated Resource Guide*
Wass, Neimeyer—*Dying: Facing the Facts. Third Edition*
Weenolsen—*Transcendence of Loss over the Life Span*
Werth—*Rational Suicide? Implications for Mental Health Professionals*